CW00392379

From Goal To Gags

The Official Autobiography of Mick Miller

– MICK MILLER –

with Steve Cowper

Foreword by Johnny Vegas

An environmentally friendly book printed and bound in England by
www.printondemand-worldwide.com

Mixed Sources
Product group from well-managed
forests, and other controlled sources
www.fsc.org Cert no. TT-COC-002641
© 1996 Forest Stewardship Council

FSC

PEFC
PEFC/16-33-415

PEFC Certified
This product is
from sustainably
managed forests
and controlled
sources
www.pefc.org

This book is made entirely of chain-of-custody materials

www.fast-print.net/store.php

From Goal To Gags; The Official Autobiography of Mick Miller
Copyright © Mick Miller and Steve Cowper 2012

All rights reserved

No part of this book may be reproduced in any form by photocopying
or any electronic or mechanical means, including information storage
or retrieval systems, without permission in writing from both the
copyright owner and the publisher of the book.

Cover Photographs by Andy Hollingworth

Special thanks to Andy Wood for his help putting this book together.

All enquiries to Steve Cowper 07734 697453
Email: mickmillercomedy@hotmail.com
Website: www.mickmiller.biz

ISBN 978-178035-455-2

First published 2012 by
FASTPRINT PUBLISHING
Peterborough, England.

Foreword

When Graham Duff, the writer of IDEAL, and series producer Gill Isles first suggested casting Mick Miller as my Dad in the show my immediate reaction was "Well he's a brilliant comic...but can he act?" Graham came back with "Well that's what people said when we talked about casting you...except they didn't add the 'brilliant comic' bit!" And so it was that Mick joined the ranks of the IDEAL cast.

Now everything I knew of Mick up until that point I'd learned from the TV. "THE COMEDIANS" was essential viewing in our house growing up, and Mick was definitely one of the stars of the show. Having gone back and watched him since with a comic's eye, I realise that Mick's genius went way beyond sending up that gleaming cranium of his that could turn Vidal Sassoon to bed wetting. I mean seriously, the rest of his hair looks like those curtains that roll around the front of coffin at a crematorium. In fact Mick's whole head resembles one big follicle memorial service. He should have hymn numbers tattooed on his forehead! But it's a look that's always worked brilliantly for him. It's the perfect foot in the door at those all-important opening moments of a gig when trying to grab an audience's attention, and why Mick had my family and I laughing before he'd even said a word.

But as I've said, going back now and watching Mick's set from a technical viewpoint, I can appreciate what I'd have taken for granted back then. Of course he had, and still has, brilliant gags. Not just the one's you've heard down the local boozer. I mean really well observed gags. They're the product of a bloke who loves people watching. He's a man who delights in pointing out the absurdities in life, but as with all truly gifted comics, Mick finds a way to laugh about them in the

1

process. He puts pain through a mincing machine and somehow produces a top quality feel good sausages of silliness. His hangdog expression screams "Oh woe is me!" but his inspired sense of humour tells a very different story.

And that's why casting Mick in IDEAL was a stroke of genius on the producer's part. Who better to play a conman Dad who can fake a terminal illness in order to rip off his own son who he hasn't seen for years, and yet still make him incredibly likeable as a character and unbelievably funny to boot? As with all the best comics, Mick could put any top thespian in the shade when it comes to portraying whimsical pathos. It's simply second nature to him, and if I had the chance now to go back now and have my pick of any other actor working today? I can honestly say, hand on heart, that Mick would be my first choice every time.

My out and out favourite routine of Mick's is the drunken radio presenter who gets increasingly hammered whilst trying to tell a NODDY story. It's sheer genius and makes me almost envious when I watch Mick perform it, as I cannot help myself wishing I'd thought of it myself. The gags are brilliant, and I just love how he incorporates the presenter's drinking into the radio sound effects. But it's the physical performance that leaves me aching from laughter. As Johnny Vegas I know a fair bit about drinking, and years spent working behind a bar had helped me hone what I thought was pretty good drunk impression. In fact my whole act hinged on the audience believing I was sloshed. And yes, I admit, sometimes the line was blurred between acting drunk, and being drunk. Either way I thought I had that performance down to a tee. But when I watch Mick I am reminded just who the monkey is, and who's the organ grinder. I have said to Mick before, in all earnestness, that his portrayal of a drunk is not only one of my absolute all time favourite comedy routines, but it is also one of the finest examples of physical clowning that I have ever seen, and every single performance makes me laugh like I'm watching it for the very first time.

It is often said that eyes are the mirror to the soul, and when you're talking to Mick you can see the mischief gleaming away in them. There's a cheeky schoolboy grin that he can't hold back no matter what the subject matter. He actually can't help or stop himself from mining the humour out of everything and anything life throws his way. For every tale I have to tell Mick has a dozen, and all of them a dozen times funnier than mine. And that is why whenever Mick's name popped up on a call sheet meaning he was going to be on set that day, then I and everyone else in production, cast and crew alike, all knew we were in for a genuine treat.

Mick was always legging it back from one gig and rushing off to another the minute he'd finished his filming. I seriously don't know where he gets the energy from, but I'm always impressed by it, as well as grateful for the constant boxes of duty free that he'd always bring back for me from one of his countless continental cruise ship engagements. Mick is generous almost to a fault, and I know he wouldn't dream of taking any money from me for them, so I've never offered him any. And I'll fight any man who suggests that I only agreed to write this introduction so I could hint to Mick that I'm running low on Marlboro Golds!

Mick is a comic's comic, and his gift of delivering a gag is no less appreciated by other comedians as it is his audiences. Testament to this fact is the amount of young up and coming comics, 'alternative' comedians as some of them like to be referred to, who have reported back to me just how brilliant he was at Manchester's XS MALARKEY club. A pub hosting a club that thrives on encouraging brand new comedians to the circuit as well as constantly encouraging established acts to come and play the room. Now no offence to Mick, but as far as that club's idea of established is concerned, that's like comparing the Magna Carter to a pile of BEANO comics. Mick was around before most of these new acts' were twinkles in their parents' eyes! But the reverence, with which they talked about Mick, and his routine, was humbling. But that's because Mick has funny bones. He's not Old School trying desperately to be New School. He's not jaded, nor is he suspicious of the way comedy has evolved since he first took to the stage, because he has always been, and always will be, bloody funny. Mick has nothing that needs to be proved to any comedian of any generation because what he does comes from the heart, and as a result he is as timeless as he is brilliant.

Showbiz can be a fickle business and as a result there is not a huge list of fellow professionals that I also refer to as friends. I have many colleagues within the industry whom I think a lot of, but I've always been wary of losing my link with those friends and family that I hold dear the most. I've met those whose whole self esteem appeared to be wrapped up in the notion of fame and the success that can come with it, unfortunately losing sight of what's most important along the way. When Mick isn't making me laugh with tales from his extensive travels, he's talking of his family. And he does so with a real genuine warmth and affection. For all of Mick's success, and everything that he's achieved that could certainly turn the heads of other folk, he hasn't lost the run of himself. That's why it was my absolute privilege to write this short foreword to accompany his book. That and the fact that I really am desperately low on Marlboro gold's. In all seriousness though, Mick Miller is a comedy legend with whom I am honoured to be able to say that I have worked with. And although he may have only played my Dad in the television series IDEAL, he has always behaved like a true comedic father figure off screen. Mick is a remarkable guy and somebody I am proud to consider my friend. Now I can't guarantee that Mick feels the same way about myself, but I wish him all the best with his story anyway, and cannot wait to read this and learn a little bit more about one of the finest ever comedians this country has ever produced.

Best Wishes Mucker!

Johnny Vegas

Ps. If they're out of Marlboro Gold, then get the Menthol, but not the Reds! Thanks

Chapter 1

In The Beginning

It all began in Dingle, Liverpool 8, on 25th February 1950. I was the second child of the Lawton family. My father, Stanley, was the manager of the mobile Co-op shop. He would drive all around the Kirkby area selling groceries to anyone and everyone. My mother, Evelyn, worked in the local high street Co-op shop where she worked on the fruit and veg counter. We weren't the richest family in the world, but we were never short of fruit and veg! It might have had bruises on it, but we just cut the bruises out.

My sister, Marilyn, was two years older than me and, as we were poor, "hand me down" clothes were the norm and didn't bother me. However, turning up for the first day at school and finding out that I was the only boy in the school wearing pink wellington boots was a bit of a shock.

My mother was a Catholic, my father was C of E and I was sent to "Mount Carmel Catholic School." I vividly remember our headmaster, Mr. Killiekelly, playing the violin at morning assembly. Most schools had a piano, but we had a violin! For fifty years I've hated the sound of the violin. But I recently saw a fabulous girl group called "Bond" on the television. Four beautiful girls playing violins. I might just get over my violin phobia now.

I took my first holy communion at Mount Carmel. My parents were so proud as they came along to witness this important event in a Catholic child's life. I will never forget standing there, dressed in my best outfit. It consisted of short trousers, long socks, a white shirt and to finish it all off, a dickie bow tie. I must have looked like a right prat! But my mother thought I looked very smart and that was all that mattered.

I was never very academic at school, and always preferred sport. I was bored in class, so I became the class joker. In fact, when I was asked what the cardinals took with them when they went in to elect a new Pope, I said "Their wives." That answer got me my first big laugh. It also got me a rap over my knuckles with a ruler: they could hit you in those days. My comedy career had begun, despite the pain.

Learning the "Three R's" was hard enough for me, but then they wanted us to speak Latin. I couldn't relate to a two thousand year-old language because in our area everyone was working class. Who ever heard anyone speaking Latin in their lunch break? Latin is not a subject that you could fall back on in later life!

The teachers did try different ways to get us interested. One way was to have religious quizzes. I did try, but wasn't very good. We were once asked why the Pope was visiting Lourdes. Well, being keen on sport, I jumped in with an answer: "He's gone to watch the cricket miss!" I got another big laugh quickly followed by the "Strap." I was getting more laughs but each time the punishment was getting more painful, but at least I was becoming more popular with my classmates.

At the age of ten we moved, and our new house was in the Wavertree area of Liverpool. So this meant moving schools. I became the new boy in the class at "Our Lady Of Good Hope School." You've guessed it, another Catholic school. Making new friends at the age of ten at a new school in a new area is not easy, but I managed, and made friends that have become friends for life. In particular, there was a family who lived around the corner from us. The Jenkins family became my best mates. They were a large family, full of big characters: nine kids in total, six boys and three girls. Finlay was the eldest He was the same age as me but he didn't attend the Catholic school. We met whilst playing football in the park. After the match, we called at the local shop for a "Frozen Jubbly" (a kind of iced lolly) and went back to his house for some pop. You can imagine what it was like, nine kids and nine kids mates! It was very full and very noisy but his parents didn't seem to mind. It was obviously a very happy home. His mum, Margaret, would often feed us all.

The shock came when I realised that they were the local undertakers. The house was next to a petrol filling station, also owned by them which in turn was next to the chapel of rest and a workshop where they made their own coffins. Jimmy, the father, was a bit of an entrepreneur. Funerals, petrol station, car wash (by hand), a boat business and in his spare time he even managed a band. He was never short of cheap labour with nine kids and a new recruit in me. It wasn't long before I was working weekends at the car wash. I got a quid a day and the cleanest hands in Wavertree. At the end of the day my fingers were as wrinkled as old prunes You'd have thought I'd just swam the Channel.

The car wash closed at five o'clock, so we would all go down the road to "Olive Mount School" where they had a hockey pitch with small hockey goals.

We would sneak in and this pitch became our Anfield or Goodison Park. The

Jenkins clan were all Liverpool supporters and I was an Evertonian but we never let that bother us. The only thing that did bother us was when the school caretaker used to chase us off. He'd always shout at us and tell us he knew where we all lived, but he never came around. We never did any damage, just played the game that we all loved. It was these early games that made me want to play professionally.

Being a Catholic was becoming a problem because all the local kids would play on a Sunday, but I was expected to go to Mass. What I really wanted to do was play in goal. The Sunday morning knock about had much more appeal than the hour-long Sunday Mass. So, when my mother asked if I was going with her to morning Mass, or the six o'clock one by myself, I would always choose the six o'clock one. When I returned from "Mass", I always thought I'd got away with it, but my mother wasn't daft. The first thing she asked was," Which priest took the Mass?" When I couldn't tell her, she would check my shoes for mud. Not only was I in trouble for not going to Mass, but I was also in big trouble for playing football in my Sunday best clothes.

At the age of twelve it was time for another Catholic school. This time I moved up to "Cardinal Newman Secondary Modern School" and was in my element when I found out that they had a school football team. Sod the lessons: let me get into the team.

I was placed in Class 1C. In those days we were streamed into A, B and C classes. Us thickies were put in the C class. I always knew that I wanted to play football and managed to get into the school team in my first year. I had finally found a reason to go to school and I threw myself into as many of the sporting opportunities as possible. P.E. and games were my favourite lessons. When the teams were picked I was never the last one standing by the wall, the one that nobody wanted. From hating going to school I was now stopping back after lessons to take part in extra sporting clubs. Anything to do with sport I was there. We played everything from football to basketball, cross-country running to trampoline. In fact the only thing we didn't play was cricket. I suppose that was because nobody in our school could afford the bat.

With all this extra-curricular activity my achievements improved, culminating with the highlight of my school life. Yes, I started my second year as a "milk monitor." To perform the duties required in this special position I had to be able to count to thirty and carry a crate. The perks of the job meant that I got fifteen minutes off lessons and loads of calcium. Also, any of the first years that upset me went without their milk ration, which was quite handy as some of the fourth-year kids were a lot bigger than me and demanded extra supplies. Milk was like the underground currency of the playground.

The second year of secondary education saw many new subjects open up but, as I was in the C class, our subjects were still limited. We were not allowed to do metalwork or science as the teachers wouldn't trust us with Bunsen burners, dangerous chemicals or sharp objects, but we were allowed to do art, pottery and painting. My paintings were in the style of "Picasso" but I wasn't even trying: I was never very good at eyes.

My school reports were slowly improving and, as a reward, my dad took me to Goodison Park to see my first floodlit match. What a reward, as it was Everton versus Liverpool! It was a great opportunity to see my heroes and Liverpool's big new signing, Ian St. John. As a twelve-year-old football fanatic I revelled in the atmosphere: the noise, the smell of smoke, beer and hot pies. I also learned a few new names for a referee. I was hooked and dreamed of playing under those floodlights.

The typical scouse humour was out in force that night and, as we queued to go through the turnstiles, I remember police on horseback using the horses to gently push and keep the queue in order. One officer shouted, "Keep in line," and a bloke in the queue shouted back, "Oi, don't get on your high horse." That line still makes me smile all these years later. Even the stony-faced copper laughed.

From that day on I was hooked on watching live, professional football matches. My parents both worked on Saturdays, so I would go to Goodison Park on my own and always arrived early. I'd try to be there by one o'clock, so that I could get a place near the tunnel. That was the prized spot to be as I could almost touch my heroes, my favourites being Alex Young, Bobby Collins, Brian Labone and of course the goalkeeper, Albert Dunlop. I felt like a king stood there, but suddenly, marching out of the tunnel before the teams, I noticed one of the school swots. He strode out looking like an "SS" officer in his first aid uniform. I've never been so jealous as he must have met the teams. It was at that point that I knew I had to be either a first aider or a professional footballer. But as I fainted at the sight of blood, my options were narrowed somewhat. With this in mind, I started to put all my effort into improving my football skills.

During the summer months, when the nights were light, my Dad would take me to the park and we'd practice like mad. He had played himself and was a reasonable goalie. So it was natural for me to learn these skills from him. It paid off because in 1964, at the age of fourteen, I was chosen for a trial with the "Liverpool Catholic Schools" team. To me, this was like winning the football pools. All I had to do was prove that I was the best schoolboy goalkeeper in Liverpool. So I turned up at "Edinburgh Park", home to the "Liverpool Dockers" team. I was a bit daunted when I arrived. There must have been about a hundred kids all wearing their school strips. It turned out that only three of us were there for goalkeeping. I tried to keep calm and remembered my father's words: "Just do your best son, I'm proud of you for getting this far". I was determined not to let him down.

The following week was agony. I never knew a week could seem so long. Would I make the squad? Eventually, the wait was over. A letter landed on the mat. My hands were shaking as I opened it, which was not good for a goalkeeper! It was good news. I was in the squad. Not only that, but my first outing would be against Manchester Schools at "The Cliff", Manchester United's training ground. The big day came and we were all on the coach for the one-hour trip to Manchester. As you might have gathered by now, even though I went to a Catholic school and had been chosen for a Catholic team, I wasn't really into the religious side of things. But I have to admit to a little prayer just before the final team was chosen. This wasn't announced until we were in the car park at "The Cliff". The one consolation was that, as a goalie, that position was always announced first. Would I be first choice goalie? Our manager stood up at the front and congratulated us all on getting this far. As expected he named his team for the match."

Firstly, in goal, we have...
...Lawton". I was in! It seemed such a long gap, rather like they do on TV shows.

The match started, and I settled into my position. The first half was uneventful, apart from the moment I missed the ball from a corner. Luckily their centre forward headed it over the bar. So, it was nil each at half-time. In the changing room that famous scouse humour came out again, when I was given the nickname "Dracula," because "I was no good with crosses!" We went on to win the game 2 – 0. We celebrated after the game, and felt just like Liverpool F.C. Now, as this was Manchester United's training ground, there was a huge communal bath. It was just like you'd always imagined. We all jumped in, shouting and cheering. How could things get any better? Well, they did. Here I was, fourteen-years-old and I was about to experience the greatest moment of my life. Bobby Charlton came into the room and congratulated us on a great game. He was a Manchester Utd. and England legend, a real role model. I wanted to be like him and thought: one day I'll have hair like him! That day reinforced my determination to make it as a professional player.

Not long after this, a new boy's club was opened in Wavertree. This was a great place to go as there were so many activities. There was everything from sport to weekend camping. I immediately joined along with Finlay Jenkins and his brothers, Richard, Jimmy and Gary. The place was very well run, and kept a lot of young people out of a lot of trouble. The nearest thing that we got to drugs was a "Beecham's Powder!" I owe a lot to Mr. O'Brien, who ran the club. He was a wonderful man. We all called him "Obi" and he was an inspiration to many of the local kids. He gave us all a chance to improve ourselves in a safe and fun environment. One of the other lads at the club, Alan Whittle, went on to play for Everton and Crystal Palace. So at last I can now publicly praise "Obi" for all his good work. I'm not sure if he is still with us but, if not, I know that if there is a heaven, he'll be keeping the angels in check.

We continued to go to the club and I learned as much as I could about playing football. At least it kept me off the streets and out of trouble. One night Finlay came in with a copy of a "Charles Buchan's Football Monthly." He showed me an article about the great Stanley Matthews taking over as the manager at Port Vale Football Club. In it there was a piece about how he was looking for new talent and how you could contact the club for a trial. We decided there and then to write to the club. Now, as Finlay was in an A class, and I was still in the C class, we thought it would be better for him to write the letter. He was a neater writer than me and his spelling was better. We posted it off and dreamed about both of us playing in the same team. We were fifteen by this time and I had given up hope of getting a degree at university. Finlay didn't want to go into the family funeral business. So this seemed like a good option.

That very same night Finlay received an urgent phone call at the club. It was his father. He needed help: a crisis had arisen. He had got a member of staff off ill and had nobody to assist in the collection of a "customer". Finlay was squeamish about the funeral business and couldn't bring himself to deal with corpses. So his dad asked to speak to me. He asked if I would help but I refused point blank. At this point in the conversation he mentioned the money that I would earn. Two pounds was a lot of money back then, so I changed my mind and agreed to do it.

Twenty minutes later, the "Black Van" arrived at the club to pick me up. Bert was driving and he was one of life's characters. He had a full head of grey hair but that day he had tried to dye it brown. He insisted he had read the instructions correctly and followed them to the letter. But here I was, sitting in a black van, ready to pick up my first corpse, with a man who had strawberry-coloured hair. He drove us back to the funeral parlour so he could get me a black jacket and tie. Unfortunately, I think this jacket must have belonged to Geoff Capes. I wasn't a big lad and the only clothes that were there were massive on me. I was nowhere near a seventeen-inch collar and must have looked ridiculous. We needed to get there and, with no other options, we set off. The address was in Childwall and, as we arrived, we realised that it was a tower block. You've guessed, it was a flat near to the top.

Bert was now in professional undertaker mode. His face was straight as he opened the back of the van. We pulled out the special coffin that was used for "pick-ups" and set off to find the lift. Luckily it was working, so we pressed for the tenth floor. Half-way up, the lift stopped, and the doors opened. Someone had called the lift to the fifth floor. As the doors slowly opened, they revealed a man who was the worse for wear, inebriated, and in fact pissed as a newt. He swayed about as he looked firstly at Bert (with his strawberry-coloured hair), then at me with my baggy clothes and lastly at the upright coffin. As we looked back at him he just said: "I'll get the next one!" It could only happen in Liverpool with the dry scouse wit. We carried on with our business, did the job and returned home. That was my first and last job in undertaking.

Two weeks to the day after we had posted the letter we received a reply. We had both been accepted for a trial for the club. A coach would pick us up at Queens Drive in Liverpool. Ironically, the pick-up point was to be just outside "Littlewoods Football Pools" offices. We would have to be there at nine o'clock on a Sunday morning in a month's time.

The big day came, and we were at the pick-up point at least an hour early. By the time the coach arrived there were about forty eager youngsters ready for the biggest day of their lives. When the coach pulled up, a man with a clipboard got off and proceeded to call out the names of all the kids who were supposed to be getting on board. "Jenkins and Lawton" were called and we boarded the coach together, and began our hour and a half trip down to Stoke. We were expecting to go to "Vale Park", but the trials were to be held at The Co-op sports field. We got off the coach and changed into our football kits. Names were called out and, for the first time ever, Finlay and I were on opposite sides. It felt odd, but I just had to get on with it and show them how good I had become. I played a blinder of a game not putting a foot wrong. I had kept a clean sheet and was really pleased with how I'd played. Had I done enough? We were all congratulated on our efforts and sent to get changed. Then it was into the clubhouse for tea and biscuits.

Finlay and I discussed the game and talked about how each other had performed. Then, a door opened and in walked Stanley Matthews accompanied by his assistant, Jackie Mudie. Everyone was in awe. After all, this man was a legend. He looked around the room and walked straight over to the table that Finlay and I were sat at. He sat down and began asking questions about me and my football. He wanted to know about my school, any teams I had played for and if I had signed any papers for other clubs. Finlay sat there and, although he looked disappointed for himself, I could tell that he was pleased for me. At the end of our chat, Stanley Matthews told me that he wanted to see me again. He left an assistant to sort out the details. Everyone else had been told that they would receive a letter telling them how they had done. I couldn't wait to get home to tell my parents what had happened. The great Stanley Matthews thought that I was a good goalkeeper and wanted to see me again. I was fifteen and had this great opportunity in front of me.

A letter duly arrived saying that I was to be given a game with the "B" Team, which meant that for the first time in my life I was no longer a "C". The game was to be in three-weeks time at the same ground as I had my trial. The opposition was to be a local colliery team but this was my first outing for a professional football club.

The day of the match arrived and my very proud father took me to Stoke in his Ford Popular. I still remember the number plate, UKF 221. I'd like to bet that number is on another car now. When we arrived at the ground Reg Burkes, the head coach, met us. He wanted to talk to my dad about signing schoolboy forms, which would tie me to Port Vale Football Club for the next six months. It was what I wanted, so he signed immediately. Full of confidence, I went to play the match. Once again, I kept a clean sheet as we won 3-0. When we got back to Liverpool my dad wasted no time in getting down to his local pub to tell all his mates about what had happened. To him, I'd just won the World Cup.

To my surprise, the following Thursday we received a phone call from Reg Burke. The reserve team's goalkeeper had been injured, so I had been picked to play for Port Vale Reserves on the following Saturday. The match was to be at Vale Park. I could hardly believe it: I'd gone from playing at the boys' club, to playing in the reserve team at Port Vale in just a few short weeks.

My dad had changed jobs and I was gutted to find out that he couldn't get time off work to take me to the match. He had just taken a job as an insurance payment collector for The Co-op, and Saturday was his big cash collection day. So, my Uncle Sid stepped into the breach and drove me down to Stoke in his Vauxhall Velux. I was nervous as we drove down. I would be playing my first game on a professional pitch, with full-time professionals. The pitch at Vale Park was one of the biggest in the country and there would be about a thousand people watching. That would be the biggest crowd I'd played in front of. It was scary, but I settled into the match. It was in this game that I lost my clean sheet, but it was to a penalty, and nobody blamed me for a mistake. We went on to win this match 2-1.

My next half a dozen matches were played for the "A" team. Yes, I was finally an "A" after years of being a "C". This was basically the apprentices' team. I worked my guts out and tried to make a good impression. One day, after a match, I was taken to one side and told that the club wanted a meeting with my dad. This was arranged, and my dad received a letter from the club, stating that a representative from the club would call at our house. I think he was as excited as me.

The day of the meeting arrived, and at six o'clock in the evening the doorbell rang. You can imagine the atmosphere in our house: it was a mixture of excitement and nerves. But nothing had prepared my dad for the shock he got as he opened the front door. He was expecting "a representative" from the club. What he got was his football hero, Stanley Matthews, accompanied by Jackie Mudie. He kept them on the doorstep as long as he could, so that as many of the neighbours as possible could see who was calling at our house. Once inside, he offered them a cup of tea or, if they fancied it, a drop of Scotch whisky. For those of you who don't know, Stanley Matthews was a health fanatic who was into eating all the right foods and never touched alcohol!

We all sat down, and Stanley Matthews explained that he wanted to offer me a two-year contract as an apprentice professional football player. My dad looked stunned as he went on to explain that if I carried on as I had started I could have national team potential. The terms and conditions were discussed and contracts signed.

For the record, football was a poorer sport in those days. I wasn't going to be a millionaire overnight. Nowadays we hear of massive wages, transfer fees and signing-on fees. I thought sponsorship was what you got for doing a charity walk. I was to get six pounds per week and my board and lodgings would be paid (another six pounds per week). When I look back at this time I still laugh because today I would have got a much better deal. But back then it was an offer that you couldn't refuse if you wanted a football career. The icing on the cake of this deal was that my mother would receive an eighteen-piece, bone china tea set. She was over the moon and said that she would keep it "for best". This actually meant that she thought that it was too good for us to use. I've never even had so much as a cup of tea from it.

I was still at school with three months to go. So Port Vale wrote to the Education Department and obtained special permission allowing me to have two days a week off. All of my mates were envious. I was getting two days off school to train and play football. Even some of the teachers seemed jealous. I was told a story about the class register being called and when I didn't answer the teacher asked where I was. One of the class replied, "He's in Stoke Sir, do you want me to go and get him?" Typical, anything to get out of lessons.

July finally arrived and school finished. No graduation ceremony for us! No parties. Most of the class just left school on the Friday afternoon and started work on the Monday morning. I, however, had a week off, and then I headed for the bright lights of Stoke-on-Trent. A new life awaited. I was no longer a kid.

Chapter 2

The Port Vale Years

With my bags packed, and my brand new, brightly-polished "Adidas" boots, I was all ready to go. My mum shed a tear and gave me a hug. You'd have thought I had been going halfway around the world, not just an hour and a half down the road! Good old dad had taken the day off work to drive me down to Stoke. No train journey for me. He gave me some fatherly advice about life away from home and how I should behave. One piece of his advice is burnt in my memory. You may wish to note this down: it might just make the world a better place. "Son," he said, "You'll probably have to go and eat in some posh restaurants. Remember, don't eat your peas off your knife." To this day, I have never eaten peas that way.

We arrived in Stoke and proceeded to find the "digs". I, Michael Lawton, was to stop at Mrs. Lawton's house in Lawton Street. In the words of the great comedian, Harry Hill, "What are the chances of that happening"? She was a lovely woman, aged about seventy. She showed me to my single-bedded room, where I left my bags. We were only there for about ten minutes, as I was due at Vale Park. My dad drove us there and we parked in the "players only" car park. I had to report to the manager's office, where Stanley Matthews met us. He welcomed me to the club, offered my dad a cup of tea and sent me off to pick up my training kit. As I returned to the office, it was time for my dad to leave. We went to the car park and said our goodbyes. He drove off and I went back into the ground.

As an apprentice I would be using the away team's changing room. So I made my way there and introduced myself to the training staff. I was issued with the training number thirty-two which had to be marked onto my kit. I was shown how to do this with a stencil and a pot of tar. The tar would not come off under any circumstances. In fact, judging by the quality of those shirts, the tar would be still there long after the shirt had gone.

After I had marked up all of my kit I changed into it. I was ready for the first proper training session of my new career. I headed for the tunnel but was stopped in my tracks. "Where do you think you're going?" boomed a voice. "I'm here for training" I replied. "No you're not son, these windows need cleaning". I looked at this man in disbelief. "I haven't come here to clean windows" I replied. He grabbed me by the ear and dragged me into Stanley Matthew's office. "Young Michael here, thinks he's going training Mr. Matthews. What should he do?" Mr. Matthews looked up and replied "Anything that you want him to!" This was my first encounter with BILL COPE, Port Vale's answer to a regimental drill sergeant. It turned out that he was in charge of the "boot room" and was responsible for all of the kits and changing rooms. I'm a quick learner, so I asked where they kept the bucket.

By twelve o'clock the windows were sparkling. I stood back and admired my work. Mr. Cope inspected them. He seemed happy and looked at his watch. "Right son, come with me," he said. We made our way to the home team changing room and entered just as the first team came in from their training session. As I stood there, they all stripped off, throwing their kits into a big pile and jumped into the communal bath. Mr. Cope had another job for me. "Pick up those kits and match them all back together," he said. They all had tar numbers stencilled onto them and I had to sort them all out and take them down to the drying room. When that was done I had to return to the dressing room and clean the bathroom. The bathroom consisted of the large communal bath, three normal baths, six showers and floor to ceiling ceramic tiles and took three of us one hour to clean. It was now about two o'clock and Mr. Cope seemed happy with things. We were allowed to go home. I thought I'd come to be a football player but had ended the day as a janitor!

The next morning I had to be at the ground at nine o'clock. I was there early: I didn't want to upset Mr. Cope. My first job of the day was to get the kit back from the drying room. Then I had to lay them out for the first team. Each player had to have everything set out, including a towel. I made sure everything was just right. I knew what Mr. Cope was like and I didn't want to upset him.

About ten o'clock that morning another new intake of apprentices arrived. Two lads from the Midlands and three from Newcastle. Should I warn them that Mr. Cope was like Captain Mainwaring (from "Dad's Army") in training shoes? My survival instincts had kicked in and I realised that he seemed to like me because I had done as I was told the previous day. I might get an easier life. It was too late anyway: he got to them first. We were all issued with sweeping brushes and sent to sweep the terraces. I was now a fully-fledged bin man. Then it was off to the bathroom for kit and cleaning duties again.

At lunch break I got talking to the new lads and found out that Alan Barker and Roger Stoate were also stopping at Mrs. Lawton's with me. The three Geordies were to stop with Mrs. Malkin just around the corner. I was to find out later that it wasn't as good there, because Ma Lawton, as she became known to us, was a much better cook. Mrs. Malkin was much more strict with them. She had a budgie, unusually called Joey, which she talked to for hours on end. I don't know why she bothered because it never talked back. In fact I don't remember it moving much. The lads became convinced it was stuffed.

The highlight of her week was "Sing Something Simple" which was on the radio every Sunday evening. The lads wanted to listen to "The Hit Parade". So Sunday evenings became a regular lads' night at Ma Lawton's. Ma used to go to the pub for a Guinness, so we had the house to ourselves. We were only fifteen and loved our music. Alan had brought his "Dansette" record player with him, so we filled our evening listening to such great bands as The Beach Boys, Everly Brothers and, of course, The Beatles. Such wild and crazy nights!

Wednesday saw the usual kit and cleaning duties, after which all six of us were told to report to Len Parton, the head groundsman. He looked like an ex-colonel, standing there with his hands clasped behind his back. He was wearing his trademark "pork pie" hat. He beckoned for us to follow him down to his shed. This was across the other side of the pitch but we were not allowed to walk across it. The pitch was his baby and it needed cutting. We all walked around the side and into the shed. This was where he stored all his machinery and we were introduced to his lawnmower. This was no hover mower: it was bigger than my dad's car and had a seat and steering wheel. This looked like it was going to be fun. Which one of us would get to drive it? The answer came soon enough, none of us. We would be using the small hand-pushed machine that had been parked right behind the big one. It had a motor and three foot-wide blades but bear in mind that a football pitch is bigger than your average lawn. It took the rest of the day to mow that pitch. I was knackered but added gardening to the list of jobs I had unwittingly taken on. Three days and I still hadn't seen a football.

Thursday morning came and so did our usual kit duty. Then, to our surprise, Len Graham, the first team coach, came in and told us to "warm up", head out and do four laps of the track around the pitch. This was the traditional start to training. At last, to our surprise and relief, we were to do a proper training session. An hour of sprints, press-ups, sit-ups, squats etc. Or as we knew it, running and jumping! Then it was off to an area at the rear of the ground for a game of football. Unfortunately, we had to play on a "cinders" covered pitch. The training staff told us that this surface was to strengthen our leg muscles but we found out later that is was really because Port Vale couldn't afford a training pitch. It might have been good for players' muscles but, as a goalkeeper, I wasn't too keen to dive for the ball on the sharp, rough surface.

We played in teams mixed with first team players through to apprentice players. The goal consisted of two traffic cones. It was quite competitive: we all took it very seriously. I let a goal in and encountered the wrath of Roy Sproson, the club captain. "You should have dived for that!" he shouted. "Do I look fu★★ing stupid!" was my curt reply. There was a moment's silence, followed by a roar of laughter from the first team squad. Even Len Graham (the trainer) had a smile on his face. It was not really the done thing to answer back to senior players, so I had now earned the reputation of the lippy little scouser and Sproson would get his own back later in the day.

Lunchtimes were spent in the "Vale Café", just fifty yards from the ground. It was owned and run by a man called Roman. He was Polish with hands like shovels and a heart of gold. The food was good and fitted our limited budget. When he brought your food his hands would dwarf the plate. They were so big they made a dinner plate look like a side plate. As a goalie I would have loved hands like that!

We returned to the ground for afternoon training and did warm up laps around the pitch. As I completed those laps I was called over by Sproson. I had seen him talking to Bill Cope but thought nothing about it. He produced a light bulb and told me that the groundsman wanted me to change a bulb in the floodlights. Apparently the second bulb from the left had blown and it was the apprentices' job to change them. I put the bulb into my pocket. There was a ladder that went up the middle of the floodlight tower. I started to climb it. Halfway up I noticed that the floodlight bulbs were looking a lot bigger than the forty-watt domestic light bulb I had been given. Then it dawned on me, I had been set up. I looked down at the gang of players who were laughing at me. I had become the latest to fall for this trick. It was the tradition to get at least one apprentice each year.

When I reached the ground Sproson looked me in the eye and said, "Yes, you are fu★★ing stupid". He had a huge grin on his face. There was no malice involved: it was just a bit of fun at the new boy's expense. Over the next two weeks training was very hard. Pre-season training was designed to get us into the peak of fitness but practical jokes were never far away. They helped to keep us sane.

We all worked hard. The apprentices carried on with the cleaning and kit duties but picking up and sorting out the kits for the first team was becoming a bit of an issue. We couldn't understand why they threw them into a big pile only to be sorted out again. We came up with the idea of asking the players to put their own kit by their own peg. This would save so much time and allow us to get finished earlier. I was chosen as spokesman to ask the players if they would do this. When they came into the changing room I stood in the middle of them all and asked for their attention. They all went quiet, a good start. I proceeded to put our request to them. They all burst out laughing. Suddenly, several players, including Sproson, dragged me over to the treatment table. I was pinned down and my shorts were forcibly removed. One of the lads grabbed a brush and a tub of "Ralgex" (deep heat muscle rub). I don't think that the manufacturers intended it for use on your private parts but that's where they put it. It hurt like mad, but that wasn't the end of it. I was thrown into the bath. Now, for those of you who have never experienced deep heat treatment of the scrotum, warm water just makes it hotter! I vowed never to be volunteered as a spokesman again.

The season arrived and I had done well enough to gain a regular place in the "A" team. We played in the West Midlands Regional League, along with teams from Nottingham Forest, Wolverhampton Wanderers, Coventry City and quite a few semi-professional teams. We usually played these matches at eleven o'clock on Saturday mornings. The First Division clubs had fabulous facilities. My first match was against Coventry City at their training ground. Coventry were a Second

Division club and had a great deal of talent in their "A" team. We were only a Fourth Division club. It was a hard match, and we lost 4-0. I was devastated. They had just run us off the pitch. Their class shone through. Throughout the match they were passing from player to player, whilst we just would kick and run. They would kick the ball, we would just kick anything, whether it was the ball or a player.

On match days we would try to get back to Vale Park to catch the home matches. As we were in a midlands league we could usually get back no later than ten minutes after kick-off. We would all rush in, trying to avoid Bill Cope. If he knew we were there he would catch us before we could get through the door leading to the terraces, where we could disappear into the crowd. His aim was to find two apprentices to make the half-time and full-time teas. We all hated this duty as it meant missing the last ten minutes of each half, and the first ten minutes of the second half. I always seemed to get picked more than the others. Len Parton, the groundsman, was also on the prowl. He would be looking for a group of us to walk over the pitch after full-time. Our mission was to find and repair divots. These were the patches of turf that had been kicked up by the studs. We would have to place them back in the hole and press them in. That was usually an hour's job for four of us.

At this point, I must mention Lol Hamlett. He was the club "physio" and for those of you who don't know what a physio is, he's the man who runs onto the pitch with his "magic sponge". He was a lovely man, always cheerful and smiling. He was religious and never swore. If he got angry, he would use alternative words. This was so funny to hear. He would never have dreamed of using the "F" word. He would use his own version, "Fizzin". We would all laugh when he said "Oh fizzin heck!" After all, bad language was part of the game. In spite of this, he was a very well-respected member of staff. He, along with Bill Cope, were former professional players themselves. They never spoke much about their playing days, but I believe that they had both played for Bolton in the 1940's.

If the first team won on the Saturday they would normally be rewarded with Monday off. No such luck for the ground staff and apprentices We would still have to be in at nine o'clock but wouldn't have to do the kit duty. Instead, there were plenty of boots to clean. We would then go onto the terraces to collect and box up, the cushions. These were available for hire on match days, so, if you had piles or a sensitive backside, you would be more comfortable on the hard wooden bench seats.

Earlier, I mentioned that Stanley Matthews was a health freak. Well, Monday was carrot juice day. The only thing he would consume on a Monday was carrot juice. Guess who had to make it, that's right, the apprentices. So now, I was a chef as well!

Tuesday saw the return to training. We would all travel in the players' cars to Leek, where we used the Leek Town F.C. ground. This was an enclosed pitch, so we could have a good, undisturbed eleven-a-side match. Unfortunately, during the week, this pitch was home to a herd of cows. We're back to the diving for saves issue here as the goalmouth was always full of cowpats! This particular day, my luck was in. As I was the third goalkeeper, I wouldn't be in goal. It was normal in those days for goalies to be made to play on the wing, where you couldn't do any damage. You also rarely got to touch the ball. As the game progressed, it was easy to forget that you were running about in cow shit, but they all seemed to forget that they had all come in their own cars and had to travel the eight miles back to Vale Park for a shower. Could you imagine today's Premiership players doing that in their Ferraris?

As the weeks and months progressed we started to take an interest in the local girls and, as fifteen-year-old boys, we would watch them going home from the nearby girls' high school. Eventually, we got to know a few of the girls and some of the local lads. Roman, from the café, had a fourteen-year-old daughter, Rosalyn, who became one of the gang. There weren't many places to go, so we asked her to persuade her dad to open the café on an evening. He agreed, so we had somewhere to hang out, drink pop and listen to the jukebox. It became the place to go. The local lads were great with us: mind you we did give them our allocation of free tickets to the home matches. We had a great time and the regular gang grew. There were about twenty of us in all and, after a while, we began to pair off into couples. One of the lads, Mel Lintern, paired up with a lovely girl called Ann. They later married and had a couple of kids. Although we had the supposedly glamorous job, it was this group of friends who kept our feet on the ground. I look back at this period of my life with fond memories. I'd love to meet up with "the gang" again and see how they're all doing. So, if any of you are reading this, please feel free to come backstage and say hello at any of my gigs. Alternatively contact me through my management (you'll find that number and e-mail address on my website). Perhaps we could have a reunion.

The season continued but, as a club, we had little success. No trophies were won by any of the teams. The season ended in 1966, and of course, the great thing to come out of that year was England's World Cup victory. As it was the closed season, I was able to watch the final at home with my dad. Everyone in Liverpool was out celebrating. It was a memorable day. The sun was shining and the atmosphere was great. I couldn't wait to get back to Port Vale to start playing again.

On our return a new intake of apprentices arrived. Any thoughts of an easier life were soon dispelled as our kit and cleaning duties were to carry on. However, this year we would be playing in some pre-season friendly matches. These were always against decent non-league teams, and were always away matches for us. Len Parton (the groundsman) wouldn't allow anybody on his precious pitch before the start of the season! Stanley Matthews always played in these matches. That would guarantee a good crowd.

Our first friendly match was against Hereford United and I couldn't believe that I was playing against the legend, John Charles, the "Gentle Giant," as he was known. He was coming to the end of his playing career but was still a formidable opponent. I was to find out how gentle he was in the first forty-five minutes. He was renowned for his great heading ability and after ten minutes of the game I came up against it. They had been awarded a corner and the ball was crossed to him. He went to head it, I went to catch it. He won! I found myself hanging three feet in the air, tangled in the back of the net. Being the gentleman that he was, he helped me down. He even apologised in his dulcet Welsh tone, "I'm sorry about that, son," he said. We were awarded a foul. To this day, I am privileged to have played in a match involving two such legendary football players. There's an old saying that "It never leaves you" and it certainly hadn't left either of them. When Stanley got the ball it looked as though it was glued to his boots. He could send the opposition the wrong way with just a glance: a true genius. With the help of Stanley we won 3-1.

The following day I was cleaning the boots when I dropped one. It bounced and rolled behind what looked like an oil drum. There were two identical drums in the room, both with cushions on the top of them. Bill Cope and Lol used them as seats during tea breaks. As I bent down to pick up the boot I noticed a sign on the drum. It read "Pure Canadian Honey". It was also dated and the drums were still sealed. They had been there for three months, unopened. They appeared to have been an unwanted gift for Stanley's health regime. I couldn't get them out of my mind.

After I had finished for the day I called at the local corner shop. A woman was buying a jar of honey. I asked Hughie, the shopkeeper, if he sold much honey. He told me that he did. That was the point that an entrepreneur was born! I asked if he could supply me with jam jars and a deal was agreed. From then on I would stay back after training as there were jars to be filled. I would supply Hughie with jars of honey, topped off with a piece of gingham, fastened with an elastic band. He would add his own label. Two weeks and ten gallons of honey later, my supply had run out. It was good while it lasted.

A few days later as Bill and Lol sat down for their usual cuppa, I noticed that the drums were smaller than before. It slowly dawned on me what was happening. The empty drums were collapsing. I was sure that I would be found out, but I never was. Bill and Lol just brought two stools to use instead. So, I offered to throw the drums out myself. They took me up on the offer and that was the end of it.

I was now full of confidence. I had got away with the honey scam and had a couple of extra quid in my pocket. So I didn't think I could be caught out with any more practical jokes. But you must never drop your guard. One day, after training, we all came back into the changing room. Being apprentices we had to wait until last to get into the communal bath. As you can imagine a bath like that cools down. So by the time we were able to use it, it was no longer hot. This particular day I made a comment about the temperature. Sproson was about to get out. "It's a bit warmer over here" he said and promptly got out. I moved across and sure enough it was warmer. I looked at the smile on Sproson's face. "Oh no!" I thought, it had dawned on me why it was warmer. I jumped out as quickly as possible. I hope I don't need to explain why but I vowed to get my own back.

There were four main practical jokers at the club: Terry Miles, Terry Alcock, Harry Poole and, of course, Roy Sproson. I really wanted to catch them out. I hatched a plan. During my career as a honey supplier, I had access to the back room of Hughie's shop. He used to make his own ice cream and always had a large supply of "dry ice". This is a special type of ice, very much colder than normal ice. In fact, you had to wear special gloves to handle it. This is what they use for that swirling mist effect on stage and TV. If it comes into contact with water it produces steam. I had a plan.

The day had come. The usual routine after training was for the jokers in the pack to dive into the bath first. It was my turn to fill the bath with hot water but I had other ideas. Using a pair of special gloves, I had brought a small supply of dry ice. I filled the bath with cold water. I waited until they were due in and sprinkled the dry ice over the surface of the cold water. To my joy it turned to steam. I stood back and looked at the bath. It really looked like a hot bath. As expected they were first to jump in. They were pretty quick to jump back out as well! Four grown men all swore in unison. I think that the words bast★★d, scouse and little were used, not necessarily in that order. Funny though it was I knew I would be in trouble. To my surprise, Bill Cope just laughed: apparently, it was the funniest changing room prank he'd ever seen. I wasn't in any trouble at all and was not given any punishment.

A month into that season came the highlight of my career. I was called into Stanley Matthews' office. He handed me a letter and said "Congratulations". I opened it. It was from the F.A. (Football Association). I had been chosen for a trial for the England Youth Team. The venue for this trial was to be "The Beachcomber" holiday camp at Cleethorpes and all expenses would be paid. It wasn't long before the word got out around the club. I was minding my own business in the away changing room when Sproson walked in. He walked straight up to me and said, "I wanted to be one of the first to congratulate you. You really deserve it." He shook my hand and I knew that he was genuinely pleased for me. I was quite moved.

The day of the trial arrived and I was called to the treatment room to see Lol Hamlett. He gave me a pep talk and reminded me that I would be representing the club. He went over to a cupboard and took out a "Slazenger" sports bag. It was like the ones used by the first team on away fixtures. On it were the words "Port Vale F.C. Number 1". I was honoured. I headed for the railway station and caught the train to Cleethorpes.

When I arrived I checked in and met the other hopefuls. It turned out that they were mostly from First Division clubs. There were four goalkeepers in all, including two from West Ham F.C. and a promising youngster from Leicester City by the name of Peter Shilton. The England youth team coach at that time was Wilf McGuinness formerly of Manchester United. We were put through our paces for several days playing different matches. After four days, we were thanked and sent back to our clubs. Our club managers would be informed of our progress and three weeks later the news came through that I had not been successful. Peter Shilton, who went on to become the first choice England goalkeeper, had beaten me. I wasn't surprised because his club keeper, Gordon Banks, had trained him. He had been trained by the best and his talent shone through.

It was back to normal, everyday apprentice duties. Port Vale were due to play Walsall in "The League Cup." It was a night match and I was asked to man the gate on "the paddock". This was an area for season ticket holders and was standing only. The club secretary offered me ten shillings to stand at the entrance to this area and take tickets. Not bad money for a few hours' work. The fans started arriving and I did my job. I only let in those with the correct tickets. As time went on, it was obvious that this match would be a "sell-out," but there would still be room in the paddock. Never one to miss an opportunity to earn an extra couple of bob, I let a few people in. A couple of coach loads, in fact. People were so happy to get in to the ground they gave me some money. I can't remember if I passed that money on to the club secretary or not. But I do remember buying a new suit!

As the season drew to a close those of us with contracts due to expire would become very nervous. Everyone feared the worst, including me. My two-year apprenticeship was nearly through. Players were called into the manager's office one by one. My turn came: it was good news, and I was to be offered a one-year professional contract, which I signed there and then. Not everyone would be offered new contracts. My good friends, Alan Barker and Roger Stoate, were given free transfers and returned to the midlands. The three Geordie lads, Mel Lintern, Stuart Chapman and Ray Kennedy, were all offered contracts. I phoned home as soon as possible. My dad was over the moon. The ploy with the peas on the knife had worked!

The summer months allowed me to return home and catch up with all my mates. I knocked about with the Jenkins lads but avoided any funeral work. Money was not a problem any longer. I couldn't believe that I was on five weeks' holidays and getting paid for it. Looking back I think that I deserved it after all the hard work I'd done over the previous two years.

On my return to Vale Park it suddenly hit me. My mates, Alan and Roger, were not around. It was weird and I missed them. I threw myself into the pre-season training regime. The first training session finished and I ran into the changing room, stripped off and jumped into the bath. When I got out I started collecting the kits up off the floor, only to realise that it wasn't my job any more. I smiled to myself and threw them all back on the floor. We had apprentices to do that!

One day, as I walked through the car park, I couldn't help but notice Stanley Matthews and Jackie Mudie talking to Stan Mortenson. I remember thinking about all three of them playing in that famous 1953 FA Cup Final. Stan Mortenson was now managing Blackpool FC. Three weeks later Terry Alcock had been signed to Blackpool for a £20,000 transfer fee. One of the jokers had left.

That season we had a very good run in the FA Youth Cup. One match would be against Liverpool at Anfield. It was to be a night match. I couldn't wait to tell my dad. Liverpool was one of the best teams around at that time and one of the biggest. You can imagine, playing in your hometown at such a prestigious ground. I can't describe my feelings as I walked down the tunnel and saw a huge sign, "This is Anfield." To this day all the Liverpool players touch that sign before they walk out onto that hallowed turf. I tried to keep my emotions in check and I ran to my goal. I threw my gloves into the corner of the net and started to warm up. It's funny, but out of all the crowd noise, I heard a scouse voice shout out, "Alright dare Lotty lad." I turned around and looked into the crowd. Sure enough, the Jenkins clan were there in force to support me. My mum and dad, sister Marilyn and her boyfriend Dave were in the stands, where I had organised tickets for them.

The game was going well until I came out to try and save a fifty / fifty ball. I dived at the guy's feet, I got the ball, but I also got his boot in my face. That was the last thing I remember about that match. I was stretchered off the pitch, suffering concussion. When I came round I was in the dressing room with the doctor. I was OK, but we lost the match 1-0.

Back in Stoke the gang were still meeting at the café. Roman must have made a fortune out of the jukebox. It was playing non-stop throughout the evenings. I was playing the field in a non-football way. Nothing serious, but a few liaisons (enough said!) Two sisters, Susan and Linda, introduced me to the joys of soul music. I became hooked on Curtis Mayfield, The Four Tops, Sam and Dave, The Isley Brothers etc. so Roman made sure that there was plenty of this on the jukebox.

One evening the sisters had a copy of the local newspaper, "The Sentinel," with them. In it was an advert for a club in Tunstall called "The Torch". Amongst the list of live acts due to appear was The Isley Brothers. We just had to go. As we were all under age, we tried to look older. The girls all dressed up and each one of them looked like a million dollars. The lads all wore suits. We thought we all looked old enough but were nervous about getting in to the club. Would the doormen spot that we were too young? We needn't have worried. It seemed that so long as you weren't wearing your school uniform you would get in.

Once inside we felt quite grown up. So, full of confidence, we all had our first alcoholic drinks. The drink of choice was cider. We had a great night, the band was excellent and we were drunk. As you can imagine we were all sick as dogs and suffered our first hangovers the next day. To this day the smell of cider makes me ill.

Two weeks later Jimmy O'Neill, the regular goalkeeper, was injured during a match. I felt sorry for him but this was my big chance. I would be playing for the team in an away match at Crewe. It was a local derby match and was on a Friday evening. On the way I sat next to Jackie Mudie on the coach. My nerves were getting the better of me and I started asking questions. I was worried about the size of the crowd, so I asked Jackie how big the "gate" would be. "About fourteen feet" was his reply. Never one to give up easily, I asked again. "How many will be in the crowd?" Jackie thought for a moment and said, "Somewhere between two and twenty thousand". This only made me more nervous. He offered me a five-shilling bet that he would be right. I took the bet. He was having a bit of fun and trying to put me at ease. It worked: I enjoyed the match, which we won 2-1. The final figures for the crowd came through, 2,155. My first team debut had cost me five shillings. To his credit, this little Scottish man wouldn't take the money off me, as he knew how big the crowd was likely to be from previous games at that ground. He had a great sense of humour.

The next game saw the return of Jimmy and I was back with the reserves. During that season I played for the first team about half a dozen times, but a problem was beginning to show itself. When I had joined the club I was five feet nine inches. Now, two and a half years later, I was still only five feet nine inches. This is quite small for a professional goalkeeper. Lol broached the subject with me and asked why I wasn't growing. I hadn't got an answer to that but I did point out that Jackie Mudie was only five feet four inches and that he scored most of his goals with his head. Lol laughed but I realised that there might be a problem with my height.

As the season went on the first team played well and went on to finish in a mid-table position. But things weren't plain sailing for the club. I still don't understand the ins and outs of the matter but Port Vale became involved in a cash scandal. A court case saw them fined for illegal payments.

Three weeks before the end of the season, those with contracts that were up for renewal were called to the office. Just like the previous year, we were all worried about our future. As I waited for my turn I kept thinking about the conversation about my height. I was called in and sat down in front of Stanley Matthews and Jackie Mudie. I half-expected to be told that I would be released but when they actually said it, I was really upset. They explained that it needn't be the end of my career: I could find another club. They wished me luck in my future and I left the office. Several other players had also received the bad news, so we all got together and decided to drown our sorrows. We went to a pub in Burslem and I still remember the song on the jukebox, Young Girl by Gary Puckett and The Union Gap. I know I'm starting to sound like Simon Bates' "Our Tune", but that's the power of music and how songs can trigger memories.

A week later I was in the Vale Café with Terry Miles and Harry Poole. They had also been released from their contracts. I was saying my goodbyes to some of my mates when Terry and Harry introduced me to a friend of theirs, Stan Smith, another ex-Port Vale player. He was now managing a team in the Cheshire League. As we talked, he told me that although Terry and Harry were reaching the end of their playing careers, he had signed them both for his team. He was also interested in signing me, giving me a chance to carry on with a career in football. I jumped at the chance and signed immediately.

Chapter 3

Working for a Living

It was time for the wanderer to return home. My parents had done well in life and had moved to a three-bedroomed house in Warrington. Dad was still in the insurance game and mum had got another job working in the local Co-op shop. They were disappointed that my professional football career had been cut short but I was welcomed home like the prodigal son.

After a few days off it was "suggested" that I visited the local labour exchange as I had no income. The younger ones amongst you will know this as the Job Centre. So, on a wet Wednesday, I caught the bus into Warrington town centre and headed into the depressing office. In those days there were plenty of jobs available. I started looking, but to my surprise, I couldn't find any vacancies for five feet nine inches tall goalkeepers! The reality of my situation had hit home. I was given an interview for a job as a warehouse man at "Nobblet and Underwood" haulage and warehousing company. The interview only lasted five minutes. I was asked if I could walk, carry hundredweight bags and count to twenty. Well, with my previous experience as a milk monitor, I knew I could easily cope with these requirements. After all, I used to have to count to thirty back then. I got the job.

I was never afraid of hard work but, after my first day, I found out what hard work really was. My working day consisted of carrying and stacking bags of animal feed. The food and, therefore the bags, really stank. Consequently, so did I. You wouldn't have liked to sit next to me on the bus home! I smelled like a pig trough.

As the weeks went on, I became more and more depressed. I hated my job and it was the closed season for football. I wouldn't be playing for my new club until mid-August. The early mornings and the heavy work were proving no good for me. Most days, I would be working on my own and would move as much as sixty tons over the day. I had to get out of this job. The final straw came when a lorry arrived carrying ten tons of cowhides, fresh from the abattoir. When I say fresh, I mean fresh, with the blood still wet. I was told to move them, but being an animal lover, the thought of doing this turned my stomach. I left the job there and then.

The following day saw another bus journey to the Warrington labour exchange. The man behind the desk remembered me as it had only been five weeks since I was there before. I could see from the look on his face that he wasn't very impressed with me being back so soon. He wanted to know why I had left the job but had to agree about the cowhides being too much to cope with. He was an animal lover too. He said that he would find me a more suitable position. After searching through his box of cards he pulled one out, rang up about it and arranged an interview for me. I got the job and became a railway man.

The following Monday I turned up at the rail yard to start my new job. I was issued with a uniform. They came in a range of sizes, extra large or massive! I chose the extra large, which was on the massive side of extra large. Whilst I was waiting for my uniform I was given the paperwork to join the union. At that time the railway was a "closed shop": everyone had to be in the union. I duly filled in my membership form and became a member of the National Union of Railwaymen, NUR for short. I was soon to find out another meaning for NUR. The lads told me it meant "No Use Rushing". I laughed but found out that they were serious. The work turned out much easier than my previous job, mainly because we didn't do very much. I quite enjoyed going to work. The "lads" were great: I got on well with everyone. Most of them were nearing retirement and just looking for an easy life, so I had an easy life as well. We had to "clock in" at half past seven in the morning, but starting work was a different matter. We had a hut with a wood-burning stove in it. It was the place we met, drank tea and chatted before working. One thing is for sure, they really knew how to chat and drink tea. Work only started when they were ready.

After three months I noticed a job advertised on the bulletin board. It was for a crane driver at Warrington Central Station. I applied and got the job. After a quick crane-driving course, I passed the test and became a fully-fledged crane driver. This was classified as "outdoor machinery" and health and safety at work was learned on the job. It consisted of shouting "Oi. Get out of the f★★king way". I was finally happy, with a job I enjoyed and I was playing football again.

My job wasn't difficult but I noticed that some people had even easier jobs. One particular bloke used to come for a cuppa with us every Friday (pay day) and then disappear off home. After a few weeks I asked someone what his job was. It turned out that his was the easiest job on the site. He drove the tractor that met the train bringing hops for Walker's Brewery in Warrington. He did this twice a day and then went home. What a job that was! My luck was changing because he was going to be off work for two weeks' holiday and I was to be his replacement. That was great, but it got better. All I had to do was meet the train, turn the hop truck around on the turntable and pull them straight into the brewery. I did this twice a day and got to claim my beer allowance, two pints a day. We were allowed to have a drink at lunchtime in those days. I could then go home.

I stayed at the railway for the next eight months, but began to get bored. There were no prospects and I didn't want to become like the older men there, just waiting to retire. By this time I was going out with the girl who lived next door, Pat. She worked part-time in the shop with my mother and was a lovely girl. We had been seeing each other for quite a while when she saw an advert in the paper for fruit picking abroad. We decided to investigate this further. It turned out to be working on a kibbutz in Israel. The thought of living and working in the sun was irresistible, so we applied. We had to attend an interview at a Jewish school in Liverpool and were promptly accepted. All we had to do was find and pay for our own flights. We were so excited but still had to tell our parents of our plans. I knew that my mother would be okay with this, but my father would be a different matter. He was still upset that I didn't make it as a football player and I knew that he would look on this as another career down the pan.

I plucked up the courage and told him of our plans. The look on his face said it all, but he was always able to come out with a comment that would sum up his feelings. He gave me one of his disapproving looks and said, "No wonder Jewish businessmen have a reputation for being able to make money, when prats like you will pay to go out there and work for them for nothing!" He had a point, but we would earn a small wage and all accommodation and food would be supplied. We talked for a while about life and seeing a bit of the world. Eventually he agreed with me and gave his blessing.

So, it came to pass, in June 1970 we boarded our "El Al" flight to the holy land. I'd never been abroad before, so the whole experience was exciting and a little bit scary. We arrived in Tel Aviv in the early evening and headed for the youth hostel where we were to stop for the night. After dropping our bags off we went out for a walk and went in search of a coffee. A short time later we came across a small bar and went in. Three attractive ladies with rather a lot of lipstick on were behind the bar. We ordered coffee and sat down at a small table. As we chatted, I noticed that we were getting funny looks from behind the bar. I looked around and noticed that Pat was the only woman there (apart from the staff). Lone gentlemen kept looking in and people kept going through a curtain made from coloured plastic strips. Our coffees arrived and the waitress said, "Do you realise where you are?" Then it dawned on me: I had brought my girlfriend to a brothel. Talk about bringing coals to Newcastle. We left pretty quickly.

After a good night's sleep we caught a bus and travelled up the coast to a place called Magal. This was to be our home for the next month. We were checked in and given a place to live. It was a small wooden chalet, where we had our own room and a communal bathroom. Our room had a wardrobe, two single beds and an ingenious fly-catching device, "Laurel and Hardy," the two six inch-long lizards that already lived there. We unpacked and made ourselves at home.

The sun was shining as we went to find the farm manager. I couldn't wait to get outside into the glorious sunshine and start picking grapes. We found his office and were given our duties. Pat was to pick grapes, I was to work in the laundry. It was ninety degrees in the shade and I was to work inside in the hot steamy laundry. I remember thinking "I've just met Israel's answer to Bill Cope".

Things weren't all bad: we had a shop. My first visit was a real eye-opener. I went in not really believing what I had been told. Everything was free. Apparently this was normal practice on a kibbutz as there were practically no wages. All that was required was that you wrote down what you had taken in a book. By this time I had started smoking and couldn't believe my eyes. There in the shop was a large barrel filled with cigarettes. I think I must have taken about three thousand, but I couldn't live with myself. I lay awake all night thinking about it. So, the next morning, I returned most of them. In fact, after smoking a couple, I returned the lot because as one of the Americans working there said to me, they tasted like camel dung. I don't know how he knew that, but I'm sure he was right.

After a week all the jobs were moved around and I became an avocado picker. Pat had move on to bananas. We had thought that we would be working together but, apparently, this is what they always did. Couples were split up for work. We worked hard and by the evenings we were both knackered. A great strain was put upon our relationship.

We had one day a week off but no say in which day that would be. My first day off was a Saturday, the Jewish holy day. I couldn't do anything or go anywhere as everything was shut. Even the buses stopped running.

Life on the kibbutz was hard but we did have fun. We met some lovely people. Quite often we would receive an invite to an evening meal at one of many families who lived there permanently. The food was always excellent and fresh. We always looked forward to these evenings. A strange thing would always happen at some point during the evening though. The man of the house would go to a cupboard, get out his AK47 rifle and go out to do his patrol of the perimeter fence. I couldn't believe it. They all seemed to keep a gun in a cupboard in their homes. It was never like that in Liverpool or Warrington.

Pat was quite an academic and was making lots of new friends. In particular she became friendly with a small group of Americans who were there to "chill out before going to Harvard University". They were very intellectual and I wasn't on their wavelength at all. They were also right lazy bastards in the fields. Pat and I were drifting apart. We didn't even get the same day off work.

The month flew by and it was time to return home. I was fit and felt the healthiest I'd been in a long time. The food had been fresh and wholesome. I'd not seen a chip for a month. I'm sure Stanley Matthews would have approved. Pat was preparing to go to university and I returned to my job on the railway. I was also heavily involved in my football. This wasn't the ideal situation for a relationship and we eventually split up. She went on to Liverpool University and we lost contact.

The football season got underway and I was playing for my new team, Sandbach Ramblers. Not as glamorous as Port Vale but I really enjoyed it. I was back with my old pals Harry Poole and Terry Miles, and playing regularly. Ironically we had to play against Port Vale Reserves and beat them 3-1. Although successful, travelling to and from Sandbach was awkward. It was twenty miles each way and I was using the service buses. I was beginning to worry about completing the season but my father came to the rescue. Throughout his life he had always had a good car and was driving a "Singer Gazelle". One evening he told me of his plan. He would sell his beloved car and buy two small vans. I would have one and he would have the other. The deal was for me to take on the payments for my van and I would be mobile at last. We took delivery of brand new, "Bedford" sixhundred weight vans and I got the red one, dad got the green one. We had consecutive registration numbers and my red van was RED 267H. It had two seats in the front and room for a mattress in the back which would come in handy later on! But for now it allowed me to play football.

We did well that season and even reached the final of the "Watney's Cup". The final was against Skelmersdale United at Rhyl. The score was 1-1 at full-time and we went on to lose 2-1 in extra time. I have to say that they had a very good team, which included Steve Heighway who went on to play for Liverpool and Mickey Burns who went to Blackpool.

Skelmersdale picked up the "Watney's Trophy" and each player received a tankard. Our turn came and we were each presented with an ashtray which had a small medal attached to it on a stem which could be spun around. We were also given a Watney's pint glass, which I still have. I've often wondered what value David Dickinson would put on these items, after all, there would only be twelve of them ever made. Wouldn't there?

The season ended and Terry and Harry decided it was time to hang up their boots and retire from the game. When I found out that Stan Smith, the manager was moving on as well, I didn't renew my contract. The summer months allowed me to return to Liverpool in my red van and catch up with the Jenkins family. By this time the father, Jimmy, had spread his business interests and bought a club. "The Cabaret Club", as it was called, was in Duke Street, Liverpool and we got in free. It was there that I saw my first live stand up comedian, Bert Cook. He was a well-known name in the Liverpool clubs and was a very funny man. So if you are looking for someone to blame for me becoming a comedian, blame Bert Cook.

I mentioned earlier, that amongst Jimmy's interests, was a boat business. When he asked us if we would be interested in a trip to North Wales in connection with a boat, we jumped at the chance. The weather was good and we set off. Myself, Finlay and Richard Jenkins were looking forward to messing about in a boat. On the way there we found out from Jimmy that it was a four-berth cabin cruiser. What we didn't realise, was that he'd bought it for scrap. It was half-submerged on a slipway and he'd already removed the engine and sold that on. Our job was to dismantle it with hammers and handsaws, burn the wood and retrieve the copper nails and screws. Also we had to carefully remove all the brass fittings and porthole windows. Jimmy gave us our instructions and left in the car. We couldn't even drive away! At least he had agreed to pay us equal shares of the scrap value. It took four weekends to dismantle and we looked forward to our payday. Unfortunately, the price of scrap copper and brass fell considerably during those four weeks. I think we earned about four pence an hour.

The summer went on and the new football season drew near. I received a phone call offering me a one-year contract playing for Winsford United, which I duly accepted. Training nights were great fun because around the pitch was a greyhound track and, after training, we would all have a bet on the dogs. One of the supporters used to own greyhounds. He was a short man with big, hairy sideburns and always used to give me one tip for the night. This was the first time I had gambled and I never lost. I would often come away from training with at least a five pounds profit. I did, however, notice that after a bad performance in goal he would avoid me and not give me a tip.

The team was having an average season. No cup runs or title races and I was becoming disillusioned. Work on the railway was becoming boring: I had nothing to look forward to. The days and weeks just blended into one. I was getting depressed. But help came from an unexpected source. The following March we had a family gathering. My cousin, Anne, noticed that I wasn't my old fun-loving self. She was concerned about how "down" I had become. She, however, was happier than I'd seen her in a long time. She had been working as a Pontin's blue coat at Middleton Towers at Morecambe and was about to go to the Pontin's camp at Camber Sands near Hastings. The entertainments manager at that camp was a friend of hers, Norman Vernon. She asked me if I would be interested in becoming a Pontin's sports host. I asked her what that job entailed. She explained that it was a Blue Coat who taught and played football and other sports to the kids on holiday. As a Blue Coat, I would also be expected to join in with the Blue Coat shows. I liked the idea and asked if she could try to get me the job. She phoned Norman and two hours later I had been offered and accepted the job. The next day I handed my notice in at the railway. Two weeks later I was on my way to Hastings. My showbiz career had begun.

Chapter 4

The Pontin's Years

May 1971, and me and the little red van set out on the six-hour journey to Camber Sands. Anne had already been there for a week, as she was the "chief hostess". This meant that she had to organise all the Blue Coat rotas and sort out the entertainment programme. She was basically the assistant to the entertainments manager. On arrival we were given our accommodation and I was to share a room with one of the other Blue Coats, a comedian / singer called Roy Jay. Over that season I was to find out that Roy was a bit of a strange character.

The following morning we all queued up for our uniform. Blue blazer, white shirt, blue tie, white trousers and white shoes. Whoever thought of that for a sports host! Just like back on the railway, we had a choice of sizes: only this time they fitted.

The entertainers on the team went to rehearsals for the various shows, whilst I went to prepare the sports equipment. During the next few days more staff arrived on site. It was a hive of activity: bar staff were filling the bars, catering staff were cleaning the kitchens and the cleaners cleaned the camp. The first visitors were due to arrive on the Saturday morning.

The big day arrived and we were called to a staff meeting at eight o'clock in the morning. Norman Vernon, the entertainments manager, issued the instructions for this important day. I was to go to the railway station at Rye and meet the holidaymakers. Pontin's had a coach to transport them all up to the camp. I just had to stand there and show them where the coach would be. The uniform commanded respect, I started to relax and have a laugh and a joke with everyone as they arrived. I really enjoyed this day as I met so many happy people.

With the first trainload all sorted out, I had time to look around as the trains arrived at three-hourly intervals. I soon found a nice little pub, full of very friendly locals. Again, the uniform was a great benefit, as everyone knew who you were and what you did. The pub was a favourite haunt of the local fishermen, which would come in handy later on.

The final holidaymakers arrived on the 5.30pm train and I was back on the camp by six o'clock. There was just enough time for a "staff meal," a quick shower and change of uniform. The evening uniform consisted of black trousers, black shoes, white shirt, bow tie and blue blazer. It was now time to report to the ballroom for Bingo.

Roy Jay used to call the Bingo and the rest of us would act as "checkers". Following half an hour of Bingo the resident band, Steve Stephenson's Show Band, would perform. It was during this performance that I found out we were all expected to dance with anyone who asked. When I say dance, I mean proper ballroom dancing, not the Northern soul stuff that I did. I would cringe as the bandleader announced the next dance and try to blend into a dark corner. But there was no escape as some of these women would seek you out. They would approach us like a Harry Enfield character, "Young man, you seem like a nice young man." They would physically drag us on to the dance floor. I hated it until I got my first pretty younger one. Suddenly, life wasn't so bad.

At ten o'clock it was cabaret time. That night it was "Zena Martell's TV Spotlights". The act was a male and female vocalist backed by twelve beautiful dancing girls. We had to sit on the dance floor and stop the kids from running in front of them. That was as close as I ever got to those girls, as they had a chaperone and were escorted to and from their bus.

Roy, my room-mate, and Norman worked in the downstairs room. It was called "The Rye Bar" and was the main cabaret room. Roy must have done well that night, because when I had finished for the night, I couldn't get into my room. We'd not been open for twenty-four hours and Roy had pulled! I had just worked a fifteen-hour day and couldn't go to bed. I had to go on a walkabout whilst he finished. When I finally got in, he just smiled and said, "You'll get your own back one day".

My first day as a Blue Coat had finished and I had enjoyed every single minute of it, except for one thing, the ballroom dancing! I'd started the evening thinking that a Volta was a type of foreign car and ended it by thinking that if it was it had just run over my feet.

The next morning we had our regular entertainments meeting. This meeting filled everyone with fear. We were told that Fred Pontin was coming to the camp. This news put everyone on edge: everything had to be just right. We were all running around with brooms up our rear ends. I went past the car park near the reception area and noticed a sign in a car parking space. It read "RESERVED FOR MR. FRED PONTIN". As a new boy I was worried about what he would think.

Would I be good enough, would he check up on what I was doing? I needn't have worried, because he never arrived. This was a trick that the camp management used to keep the staff on their toes: he was never coming to the camp on that day.

My first job that day was to assist Roy Jay with the morning ramble. Sixty holiday makers going for a walk, how boring! We had to take them down to the beach, walk across a few sand dunes, and visit a pub and a gift shop. All this and be back by twelve o'clock. It started to rain at lunchtime, so the afternoon entertainment programme was changed to the wet weather programme. That afternoon was to be "Cine Racing" which was a new thing to me. We had reels of American horse races on cine film and the audience would bet twenty pence on the outcome. It was great fun and everyone enjoyed it.

The evening was much the same as the night before, except that I would be working in the Rye Bar. As this was the main cabaret room it attracted a younger audience than the ballroom. The Blue Coats were expected to mix with the guests a great opportunity to meet the younger ladies. But I think we had one or two young chaps on the team who were "friends of Dorothy's" and preferred meeting the younger gentlemen, if you catch my drift. Roy Jay definitely wasn't one of those! But I did get into our room that night.

Monday saw me hosting my first proper sporting event. Each week we had a table tennis exhibition with the former champion, Chester Barnes. He was brilliant and a really nice person. We would become great friends over the season. He would bring a partner and we would set up a table in the ballroom. They would play an exhibition match and show everyone some trick shots. Then, Chester would offer to play against the holidaymakers. We would always get some serious amateur players there, including county players. Some even brought their own bats. Chester would ask them if they were good players. Invariably, they said that they were. He would challenge them to a game and offer then offer them a ten-point start. He would also use a spoon instead of a bat. I never saw him lose. I still see him from time to time. He is now an assistant to Martin Pipe, the racehorse trainer.

Tuesday was wrestling day. My job was to introduce the wrestlers and try to be serious, which wasn't easy when I had to introduce "Butch", "Tarantula" and "The Headbanger". I don't think that those were their real names. They would all arrive together in a Transit van, put up the ring, then beat seven bells of shit out of each other. They would then take the ring down, pack it in to the van and head off to do it all again somewhere else in the evening. They were a great bunch of guys and before the end of the season I would become part of their show.

Wednesday was "Donkey Derby" day. This was a potentially financially rewarding event. I had noticed that although a different numbered donkey was winning each race, the winning donkey was beginning to look familiar. I was sure there was money to be made on the betting, but would have to work out a way of doing it, as I wasn't allowed to bet.

Thursday was my favourite day of the week. It was "Watney's Red Barrel" football day. The day culminated in a "final" where the runners-up each received a Watney's Red Barrel key ring and the winners each got a voucher for a pint of Red Barrel. I was in charge of the vouchers and felt another scam developing. That night was the "Blue Coat Show" where the whole team except me would perform, because I was on ballroom duty, doing the Volta and the Foxtrot.

Friday arrived and it was my day off. After a long lie in I discovered that lots of people had enjoyed their holiday and wanted to buy you a drink. As it was my day off I could accept and by teatime lots of people had thanked me. I only accepted a drink to be sociable and by the end of the night I was so sociable I fell over. But I was always ready and capable for work the next morning.

About four weeks into the season, just as I had become settled in and was starting to enjoy myself, Norman Vernon announced his resignation. I was shocked and to this day I have no idea why he did it. Anne decided to resign in support of him along with five others, including Roy Jay. She advised me to stay as most of those who resigned had other ways to earn a living. I took her advice and the following Saturday I joined the Blue Coat line up with the three others who had stayed. Help was on its way from head office in the shape of Pat Braden. He arrived during the evening and turned out to be a lovely, warm Irishman. He was an assistant manager at one of the other camps, but had been a singer and entertainer, so was the saviour that we needed.

With the shortage of Blue Coats I was asked to take on the duties of a presenter. This had its advantages: I was to present the weekly "Miss

Pontin's" competition. There would usually be about twenty pretty girls and I could ask them all the questions any young lad would want to ask. At the end of the competition, I would know how old they were and which ones were single. I loved every minute of that job, but unfortunately, I also had to host the "knobbly knees" competition and the "glamorous grannies" events.

With Roy gone, I had to go solo on the rambles. The first time I went out on my own, there must have been about seventy people. We set off over the dunes and arrived at the pub. Once everyone had been served I sat back ready to enjoy my drink. The landlord came over to me and asked where Roy was. I explained that he had left and that I was now in charge of the ramble. He shook my hand and passed me a five-pound note. I must have looked blank as he said "Remember to bring them in here." It slowly dawned on me that Roy must have had an agreement with him. I accepted and promised to keep on taking thirsty ramblers there each week. The gift shop was next on the walk and the same thing happened. I'd been out less than two hours and I was ten pounds better off. Not a bad few hours' work considering that I only earned eleven pounds a week.

I had been thinking about the donkey derby and had hatched a money making-scheme. As I said earlier, I noticed that the same donkey would win most of the races, even though the number kept changing. During the previous few weeks I'd got friendly with the donkey man. The donkeys could be temperamental, but he would always know which one was in a good mood and liable to win. He would always tell me, so all I had to do was get a bet on. As a Blue Coat, I wasn't allowed to bet on these races. So, I used to find a friendly family and ask them to put it on for me. Of course, they would be advised to place their money on the same donkey. Throughout the season I must have averaged five wins out of six races each week. My weekly earnings were improving.

Most evenings I would be working in the Rye Bar and had noticed that all the food outlets closed by 10.30pm. The bar didn't close until one o'clock. I don't know about you, but when I've had a drink, I get hungry. So another plan was hatched. On my day off I went into the town and visited the pub. As usual, the fishermen were in there. I asked them about seafood and where I should buy it in bulk. They sent me to the wholesalers, where I was able to purchase large jars of cockles and mussels. I took them back to my room and then went to the kitchen. Quite often, they would serve frozen mousse to the diners. The plastic pots that they came in would just be thrown away, so I asked if they could put them through the dishwasher and save them for me. I took them back to my room and filled them with the cockles and mussels. Whilst I had been in the town I bought a white coat and a white straw hat. That night at half past eleven, I put on my coat and hat and took a tray of seafood into the bar. I had been learning a lot about performing, so I marched around singing "Cockles and mussels alive, alive ohhh". I sold the lot. Another money-making scheme was born.

Wednesday nights were comedy nights and the regular guest was the legendary London comedian, Jimmy Jones. I would always watch his act and try to pick up tips, as I wanted to add more comedy into my presenting work. Jimmy was famous for his "Kinell" catchphrase. He insisted that he was saying "Blinking Hell" but his accent made it sound like "Kinell." It also sounded more like another, much stronger phrase. He would always "paralyse" the audience and got many standing ovations, but he never let it go to his head. He would always spend time with me after his act and give me advice on how to be a stand-up comedian. He gave me the confidence I needed to try adding comedy to my presenting. I owe this man a great deal as he set me out on the road to where I am now.

The season rolled on and things were running smoothly. The regular visiting acts were always made welcome and became close friends. My money-making schemes were all going well and I had made sure that nobody was suffering because of them. I have to say, I never robbed anyone, especially the Pontin's Company.

I began to look forward to the wrestling as the lads had offered to teach me some moves. Each week I learned a bit more and they taught me how to take a fall. We came up with the idea of them dragging me into the ring and knocking me about. Then one of them would pick me up and throw me into the corner. We never realised the effect that this would have on the audience. As a Blue Coat, they looked upon me as their friend and took it personally. When I got thrown into the corner, they went mad. Little old ladies turned into umbrella-wielding mad women. Then the missiles started. I wondered what they were throwing as some hit me and they really hurt. I couldn't believe that what they were throwing were sugar lumps. After this experience we worked on the routine and it became a regular part of the wrestling show. The audience loved it and I got to do a bit of acting.

My love, or should I say lust life was going well. A combination of that Blue Coat and a beauty contest gave me a good start. Since Roy left, I had the room to myself and I wanted to make use of it. I used to bring girls back for "liaisons" but never thought about my sideline. My room was also my storeroom: I had cockles and mussels under my bed and had become used to the smell, but it must have smelled like Billingsgate Fish Market in there. No wonder I didn't have a good repeat rate!

The season was going well after the slightly shaky start due to all the resignations and the team were now bonding. I had become good friends with John Sharman, the resident DJ. He was a northern soul fan and had a huge collection of rare discs, but couldn't play them at Pontin's. He had to play the usual chart hits and the daft party dance songs. The "Slosh" was very popular, but nowadays it's evolved into "Line Dancing". Unfortunately, the Blue Coats had to do the "Slosh" with the guests every night. For those of you not familiar with the "Slosh", you stand in a line and kick your legs up and down together with everyone else. Add to that a bit of clapping and there you have it. We were like a bunch of robots.

John and I had some good nights out and had plenty of "fun" with female guests. He was from Bournemouth and one week his parents came to the camp for a short break. Jim and Vi were great company and we would become good friends over the next year.

October finally arrived and the season was drawing to a close. The last week was known as "Finals Week" as all the guests who had won heat finals returned for the grand finals. It was a week full of knobbly knees, glamorous grannies, singers and, of course, Miss Pontin's. Throughout the season I'd hosted the Miss Pontin's contests and had got to "know" many of the winners. I never gave Finals Week a second thought. Suddenly, they were all there, in the same room. I had to lie low all week. The best-looking girls were all there: they were all looking for me. It should have been the climax of the season (if you forgive the pun) but I had to avoid meeting more than one at a time. I was living like a monk. I managed to get through the week unscathed, Saturday arrived and the season ended.

Sunday morning, I loaded my worldly possessions into the little red van and returned to Warrington. Mum couldn't do enough for me: she was so pleased to have me back home. I enjoyed being spoilt again, but I had itchy feet. I'd had a taste of show business and I wanted more.

During that week I caught up with my mates in Liverpool. It was great to see them, but many were either courting or even married. I had some serious thinking to do. By the end of the week I had made my mind up. John Sharman had told me about the entertainment scene in Bournemouth. He had always said that there was plenty of work there as the hotels operated all year round. It was an opportunity that was to good to miss. A phone call to John helped me finally make up my mind. He offered to help me get "gigs". When I told my parents I got another of my fathers disapproving looks. He had wanted me to find a "proper" job. By now I was used to this and knew that he would give me his blessing eventually. He did and two weeks later I headed to Bournemouth.

I arrived in Bournemouth with nowhere to stop. My little red van came to the rescue. I parked up in the car park at the local swimming baths. My idea was being able to get a shower there in the morning. The next day I met up with John and another ex-Blue Coat called Chris Saint. Chris had an idea to open an entertainments agency and I was to be his first act. This was all very well but he hadn't got any bookings for me. I slept in the van again that night.

We met up everyday that week and Chris would give us a progress report. He had been ringing agents, clubs and hotels, anywhere that might book a young comedian. But there were still no bookings. I had become a regular at the swimming baths and money was running low. I was too proud to sign on the dole: I wanted to make it on my own.

After a week John realised that I didn't have anywhere to live. He made a quick phone call and sorted out a room for me at his parents' house. I must admit that I was relieved. That van was bloody cold at night. Jim and Vi became surrogate parents to me. They were just setting up a business and money was a bit tight but I was able to help them. The business was a "china" shop and I had good contacts in Stoke-on-Trent, the home of pottery. I was happy to help.

Jim had bought an old bread van and converted the back of it to carry chinaware. It was fitted with a governor, which only allowed it to go fifty miles per hour. Jim, John and myself took turns to drive it the six-hour journey up to Stoke, where Jim would buy stock. Then it was a six-hour drive back to Bournemouth. The only jokes I was telling were the ones in the van to make the journey seem quicker. But this was soon to change. Chris finally got me a gig.

I remember him phoning me with the details. It was at a hotel in Boscombe. They wanted two half-hour spots and the fee was twenty pounds. Which was all very well but I only had about twenty-five minutes of material. I had no idea how I was going to make this last an hour. When I arrived I went to look at the room: it was full of elderly people. The time arrived and I had to go on stage for my first spot. I needn't have worried: they were a great audience. They were a bit slow but that went in my favour and with a few ad-libs, I managed to do the two half-hour spots.

Slowly, work started to come in. John was getting regular Friday and Saturday night work with the disco, but Christmas was getting closer and I still hadn't got any bookings for that period. So, John and I decided to go and look for some. We travelled to Weymouth to try our luck with the hotels. John would go in and ask to speak to the manager. He looked the part, as he carried a briefcase. He was a good salesman and I was booked for Christmas Eve, Christmas Day and Boxing Day at The Prince Regent Hotel in Weymouth. I was over the moon and my fee was sixty pounds for the three days.

Christmas Eve came and I drove to the gig. There was a five-piece band on as well. I introduced myself to them and asked about the audience. I hadn't thought about everyone being there on a Christmas break. It would be the same audience for each of my performances. I wouldn't be able to do my twenty-five minutes of stand up comedy three times. So, I reverted to my Pontin's training. I did bingo, competitions and a bit of comedy. After the first night the hotel manager summoned me. I feared the worst, but to my surprise, he complimented me on my performance and asked if I was available to work for him on New Year's Eve. You bet I was! I now had a gig on the best paying night of the year: I was to be paid sixty pounds for the one gig.

The New Year's gig was great. Everyone had a good time and lots to drink. My job was easier because they were all in the party mood. I couldn't believe that I had earned one hundred and twenty pounds in just a few days, but that would have to last me six weeks, because that was when I would next work.

During the time off we would kill the boredom in different ways. Then, one day, we came up with the idea of finding me a new "stage name". I was still Michael Lawton and thought it wasn't memorable enough. We weren't having much luck: ideas were thin on the ground. Then we came up with a bright idea, the phone book! The idea was to open the book at a random page and stick a pin in it. That would be my new name. Unfortunately, I didn't think I'd go very far being called P and O Ferries and after several more attempts we decided to stop using the pin. I liked being called Mick, so it was just a case of finding a suitable surname. We tried different names, but wanted something that would roll off the tongue. Something beginning with "M" would be good. After trying several surnames, we settled on Miller. Mick Miller seemed to work best, so that's what I became. For those of you who are wondering, I'd never heard of the racing greyhound, "Mick The Miller", but it was a lucky name for him and I hoped it would be for me.

The winter months were hard but, slowly, the gigs started to come in. One thing in our favour was that we could supply a night's entertainment with a comic and disco. Between us John and I made a living. I was working in the china shop during the day and doing the gigs at night. This, coupled with the trips up to Stoke with Jim to buy and collect the stock, kept me busy.

The Pontin's season was fast approaching and I had been accepted for a second season at Camber Sands. John was all set to return as the resident DJ. I was looking forward to getting back there and having fun. John had told me he felt the same. But just before we started back, John dropped a bombshell. He had been offered a job on the QE 2 as the resident DJ. It was an opportunity that he felt was too good to miss. I have to agree I'd have done the same in his shoes. So, I went to Hastings, he went to Hawaii or somewhere equally exotic. I wasn't jealous, well, not much. We kept in touch and to this day we are still friends.

Chapter 5

Onward and Upward

The long winter months had finally come to an end and I returned to Camber Sands, this time, on my own. A year before I had been the nervous new sports host but this year I was coming back as the main comedy presenter. I had become Roy Jay! The accommodation was allocated and I was given a chalet of my own. What a result. Nobody to lock me out or ask questions about the fishy smell.

After settling in I headed off to the ballroom to meet the new intake of staff. None of the old gang had returned, so I become the only Blue Coat with experience. Even Tony James, the entertainments manager, was new to Pontin's. I was the only one who knew the ropes and was already thinking of ways to add to my weekly salary. The pub was still there, as was the gift shop and the cockles and mussels were still readily available.

Tony was about to allocate the jobs and I had to make sure I would be in charge of the ramble. It wasn't difficult, as it became apparent that he had no experience in this line of work. In fact he admitted that he had only got the job because he had put a good letter together. He needed all the help he could get and I was the one he turned to. Needless to say I got the ramble, the donkey derby and the wrestling. I also managed to get a twenty-minute spot in the Blue Coat show. I could see a good season ahead.

Together, Tony and I went through the entertainment programme. Most of the visiting cabaret acts were new to the camp, although I was pleased to see that Jimmy Jones was back again. Everything was sorted out and the first guests arrived on the following Saturday. One of the new blue coats met them at the railway station and I greeted them at the camp. I was soon back in the swing of things.

Tuesday night was comedy night and that meant the return of Jimmy Jones. I was looking forward to seeing him and he was pleased to see me. He was keen to know what I'd been doing over the winter months. I told him about Bournemouth, the work over Christmas and the New Year's Eve gig. He was interested and asked if I still wanted to make it as a comedian. I told him that I was hooked and it was the only thing that I wanted to do. He was very encouraging and asked when my day off was. I told him that it was Wednesday this year. He then told me that he would be working at a pub in Peckham the following Wednesday and asked if I could get there. I thought, "Great, a chance to see "The Governor" work in a different venue." But that's not what he had in mind. He was offering me the chance to be his support act and do twenty minutes of stand-up comedy.

That night I returned to my chalet and started to work out what material I would use. I was excited but nervous and couldn't sleep very well for the next week. It was one of the longest weeks I can remember since my football trial. Eventually the day arrived and I drove to the Montague Arms in Peckham. I arrived at eight-thirty as arranged and met Jimmy. He told me that I would be on at about nine-thirty and I would only have to do ten minutes.

Jimmy opened the show and went down a storm. He introduced a girl singer who did several songs. Then it was my turn. Jimmy introduced me and I bounced on to stage. Those ten minutes seemed even longer than the week that I had been waiting. There's a phrase used by comics, and I now knew what it was like to "die on my arse". My arse had never been died on before, so it was even harder to take. I was so downhearted, Jimmy came over to me and said, "They're a hard crowd in here," and he realised that I just wasn't ready yet. I drove back to Camber Sands and back into the safety of that Blue Coat. I'd learned a lot that night.

The following week Jimmy arrived at the camp with words of comfort and encouragement for me. He explained that he thought I had what it took to be a comic, but I still had a lot to learn. He told me that that audience was one of the toughest on the circuit and not to give up. Just learn from the experience. Things would come right for me.

The very next day, rumours were flying around that Bridie Reed was coming to the camp. She was the entertainments co-ordinator from head office. Sure enough, she turned up and wanted to see me. I was worried that she may have something to say about my scams. In fact, what she had to say knocked me for six. She was moving me on to another camp, Osminton Bay near Weymouth. They needed a new presenter and had asked for me. I was shocked: what about my money-making schemes. They were giving me an extra two pounds per week but I would lose at least ten pounds from the ramble and more from the seafood sales. That wasn't all: I had started seeing Gill, a very attractive Blue Coat. So, that relationship was cut short.

By the end of the week I had packed my little red van and travelled to Weymouth. The assistant manager, Pat Braden, greeted me. All was becoming clear, because after his previous season as the replacement entertainments manager at Camber Sands, he had picked me to work with him again this season. I knew then that everything would be fine. I was introduced to the entertainment manager, Roger Layton. He was a singer and accordion player, so no threat to my act.

During the course of the day I met most of the other Blue Coats, including Jason Collins. He was from Liverpool too and was a right character. He smoked sixty fags a day, only had one lung and was five feet three inches tall. He was a singer and banjo player. What a double act him and Roger would have made! We instantly became friends.

My first evening on duty I noticed that there were no children in the room. I hadn't realised that this was Pontin's first adult-only camp. I met the band and prepared myself for the ballroom dancing with old ladies. They smiled and told me that the camp attracted groups of young, single girls and lads. I couldn't wait to get out there: after all I was wearing the ultimate pulling device, the Blue Coat. I wasn't disappointed. It reminded me of my football days, scoring away from home every night! But that wasn't all I wanted. I was always looking for ways to earn extra money.

I was working in the "Sun Lounge" which was a smaller venue and was a short walk away from the main complex. It was a great room to work and I had noticed that the management never went in as it was too far for them to walk. Once again, all the food outlets closed early, which was ideal for my cockles and mussels. I found a supplier in Weymouth and was in business again.

One downside to this camp was that it was a "catering camp" and had a restaurant for the guests. We had to greet them for breakfast and be funny at eight o'clock in the morning. Many a time I would go straight there from a chalet that wasn't mine, if you get my drift. I hated this part of the job but at least Eddie Stamper, the catering manager, was good to us. We always got a nice breakfast out of him. He was another "scouser" and we clicked immediately. I always went into the kitchen and had a laugh with all the catering staff. They were a good crowd, so I arranged to have a staff football match at least once a week. This became the place for everyone to have fun and let off steam.

One evening I called into the kitchen for a cup of tea before work. I couldn't help but notice Gary, the chef, throwing meat away. I asked him why he did this. He told me that head office insisted that each diner should have a piece of roast meat that was no smaller than six inches across. The ends of the roast joints were always less than that, and had to be thrown away. Never one to miss an opportunity, I asked if I could buy these waste pieces of meat. He said I could have them for nothing as they were just being thrown out. He asked why I wanted them: I had to be honest with him and told him my plan. Not only would I be selling seafood, I would be adding beef sandwiches to my menu. They were very successful. In fact, the band would advertise my food, not realising that it was nothing to do with Pontin's. I did so well, even the seafood supplier was impressed. He told me that I was selling more seafood than the fish stalls on Weymouth prom. He wanted to know where my shop was, but I never told him.

I managed to get on the ramble, thinking that I could repeat my pub and gift shop earnings, but this wasn't to be. The ramble had to go across the cliff top and down into Weymouth, where we would end up at another Pontin's camp called Riviera. So, no bribes there! At least I would have the chance to meet some new female Blue Coats. How wrong could I have been? Riviera was like a hotel and only had two Blue Coats: the youngest must have been about sixty-eight. You win some, you lose some.

Friday was my day off and I had come to an agreement with some of the kitchen staff. Each Thursday they would borrow my van and drive up to Dorchester and buy Scrumpy Cider. Apparently, it was stronger and cheaper than the local stuff. After work on Thursday evening we would party in the staff chalets. A prize was put up for the person who could manage to drink a gallon of cider: nobody ever claimed that prize, as it was so strong. I could use the Friday to recover and wouldn't get up until late. As I walked past the other staff chalets I used to smile at the rows of mattresses laid out to dry. It's funny how this cider made so many bladders weak.

Jason also had Fridays off and would try to get to Bournemouth as he had a girlfriend there. Some weeks I would take him in my van. Whilst he was seeing his girlfriend, I would go to Poole and visit Vi and Jim. John was still on the QE2. I noticed that there were quite a few army camps in the area and wondered about the possibility of getting some gigs in them. I contacted a few agents and was soon offered some Friday night gigs. I could earn forty pounds for a half-hour spot, so I was earning a decent amount of money per week, and had the chance to develop my comedy act.

As the season neared the end, Jason asked me what I would be doing through the winter months. I hadn't got anything planned. He told me that he was going to Bournemouth to work at a bingo club and asked me if I would be interested in a job as well. I thought about it and realised that I could still work my gigs with this job. Jason had a word and I was offered a position as a "caller." I would work the day shift and as many evenings as I wanted. It was ideal, so I accepted. We used our day off to go flat hunting and I found a bed-sit in Landsdown Road, Bournemouth. I was now financially sorted out for the winter.

I had been careful with my money throughout the season and had saved quite a bit of money. I decided that it was time for a treat. I'd always fancied myself in a sports car and now I could afford one. After looking around the dealers I settled on a new MG Midget in yellow. I felt great when I did the deal with the salesman. He looked at my van as a part exchange and I'm sure he didn't think I was a serious buyer. He changed his mind when I pulled out my wad of cash to pay the balance. His face was a picture but not nearly as much as the camp manager when he saw it.

I'd had the car for two days and I could see the camp manager was bursting to find out how I could afford to buy a sports car. Finally he asked me what my parents did for a living. He thought maybe they had paid for it. He couldn't contain himself any longer and asked outright "How could you afford that?" My smug reply was "Initiative!" but he wasn't leaving it there He smelled a rat. I had to come clean and explained that I hadn't robbed anyone, especially Pontin's. He looked blank, so I took him to my chalet and showed him my jars of cockles and mussels. I explained about my seafood business. He shook his head and smiled, "I have to hand it to you" he said "you're right, nobody has lost out here, least of all, Pontin's". He shook my hand and congratulated me, nothing more was said.

With the season finished I had to pack everything into my new car. I quickly found out that red vans hold lots more than yellow sports cars. It was a good job that the band from the camp was travelling to Bournemouth in their van and had enough room to take my things with them.

We turned up at my new flat and unloaded my stuff. I hadn't got any time to waste as I started my new job at The Vogue Bingo Hall on the Monday morning. Although I had called bingo at the holiday camps I was a bit nervous. I knew that these would be serious players and I wouldn't be able to mess around. I quickly realised that the daytime players were mainly old-age pensioners and I had to call it very slowly. If I went too quickly for them they would soon let me know. The games were for two pounds a line or four pounds for a full house. Not much money but a lot for some of the pensioners.

Jason already knew the ropes as he had worked here previously. He let me do the cash games, whilst he did the prize bingo. We would occasionally swap around but I was happy with that arrangement. I have to admit that the ladies did frighten me a bit but they soon mellowed as they got to know me. I realised that they were just like the guests at the camps and enjoyed a bit of fun. I was in my element: I would have a laugh and a joke with them. They became friends and I was always worried if one of them didn't turn up at their normal time. Many of them were only there for the company and would happily give me a pound tip out of their four pounds win. I had some happy days there.

Thursday was the serious player's day. It was the day of the "Big Link Game" where five bingo halls were linked up by a phone line and played with each other for a five hundred pound prize. We couldn't mess about on that day but I always smiled as the link-up was established. It was like the Eurovision Song Contest. "Andover, are you there?" they would reply with "Andover calling, I can hear you Bournemouth". It just made me laugh. We had to go through this routine with all the different halls, which took longer than the game.

By now, I was being offered a lot of comedy work with an agency based in Salisbury. Ace Entertainments was run by Tony Morton, who had contracts to supply entertainment to many of the army camps in the area. Most of the work was on Friday and Saturday evenings, which suited me as I could still work six afternoons at the bingo. Add the two cabaret spots to this and I was making a good living. My rent was only eight pounds fifty pence per week, so I had plenty of spare cash.

My act was improving but I really needed to work more to gain confidence. Gradually, more work came my way and I even picked up a regular Monday night gig at the Water's Edge Hotel in Bournemouth. I really enjoyed those Mondays as I could try out new material without fear of the wrath of "squaddies". If they didn't like you they would throw empty beer cans at you: a bit like that scene in "The Blues Brothers" but without the chicken wire.

I felt that I was becoming a stronger performer and wanted to spread my wings. Southampton was only about forty miles down the road, so I asked Tony Morton to try and get me some work there. I was over the moon when he phoned to tell me he had not only got me a gig, but it was a special gig. One of the clubs was having a special evening and had booked a big star to appear. He had managed to get me on as the support act. It was only twenty minutes but I would be working with a big star. Could this be the break I was looking for? I asked who the big star was; "Nicholas Parsons" was the reply. I was dumbstruck. Tony was quite pleased with himself for getting me this gig but I was left wondering just what Nicholas Parsons actually did!

I arrived in Southampton for this "special gig" and found the club. After parking my car I went in and introduced myself. Nobody was really bothered about me, not when Nicholas Parsons was there. I went to the dressing room and finally met the great man. I really didn't know what to expect but what I found was a true gentleman. He was a very nice person who took the time to talk to people. We chatted until it was time for me to go on. I had picked my best material for the twenty-minute spot and went down really well. I decided to stay and watch Nicholas do his spot. I thought he was really clever as he told his witty stories. I thought he was very good but he was not in the right environment. He was more suited to after dinner speaking than a workingman's club audience. I think the audience felt the same way but at least they had enjoyed my act.

A few days after the Southampton gig Tony called to tell me that, as a result of that night, I was being asked for by name. He had work for me all around the area. Finally, I was breaking through. It was at this time a new club opened in Bournemouth. "The Maison Royale" was a classy cabaret club attracting big names on the club circuit. Most of these were brought down from the north. I did some homework and found out that the manager was David Lever, the very same man who had given me my first Pontin's contract as a sports host. I made an appointment to see him. He vaguely remembered me but only as a sports host. I explained about my comedy act and offered to work one night for free on the understanding that if I went down well he would give me a full week's paid work. He agreed and I was put on as a support act to the singer / impressionist, Faith Brown.

The night of the gig arrived and I turned up at the club knowing that I had it in me. I was sure I could impress the manager. No sooner than I came off stage there he was in the dressing room. He had enjoyed my performance and before Faith Brown had even taken to the stage, he had offered me a week's work as the support act to an up-and-coming star, Joe Longthorne. He was a big name in the clubs in those days and was hugely talented even then.

At the end of the week David Lever called me into his office for a chat. He explained that he thought I was wasting my time trying to make it as a comedian in the Bournemouth area. I should move back up north as there were more opportunities to work up there. He was very respected in the business and I couldn't ignore his advice. The only problem I could see was that I had a flat and a bingo-calling job in Bournemouth. If I gave all this up to go up north and I couldn't get any work it would be a waste of time. David offered to find me a respectable agent who would look after me, so I agreed to give it a try. Within a week he had put me in touch with Stuart Littlewood of Stuart Littlewood Associates. Almost immediately I had contracts for six months' work. So, I gave a month's notice on my flat and at the bingo hall.

Things were starting to happen for me and I had to adjust my life. Firstly, the sports car had to go, as it was impractical for carrying any gear about. I traded it in for a "Singer Vogue" which was a much more practical car. Then, I made arrangements to move back in with my mum and dad. They had recently moved back to Liverpool and would be more than happy to have me there. I think mum just wanted to fuss over me.

As soon as I moved in the work started and I was kept very busy. The quality of work I was being offered was far better than anything I'd done before. I would not only work in clubs around the Liverpool and Manchester area but would get a whole week's work in major cabaret clubs throughout the country. Anywhere from "Caesar's Palace" in Luton to "The Sheffield Fiesta." I was supporting such acts as "The Three Degrees", "Lulu" and "The Drifter's". This was the early seventies when "The Drifters" were really "The Drifters" and not just another bunch of blokes who called themselves "The Drifters". In fact when I was abroad the other year I saw some "Drifters" who were white!

When I moved back up north I trusted David's judgement but I just hadn't realised how good Stuart Littlewood's office actually was. They looked after me very well and I got to know some of their other acts. The legendary Bernard Manning, Stu Francis and Cannon & Ball were all with this office and getting good, regular work.

I just got on with the gigs that were given to me and worked my way through the six months of contracts. I was going down well everywhere I worked and was sure that Stuart would continue to get me work. Then, one day, I received a phone call from him. He wanted to offer me three months' work in South Africa. I was stunned and asked about the gigs over there. I was told that Stu Francis was going out there and most of the decent acts from his office had done it. So, after thinking about it for a few minutes, I agreed. I'm now older and wiser and now realise that any agent worth his salt will never tell an act that a gig is crap!

Everything was sorted out for me, all the paperwork and visas were organised through the office and I received my tickets through the post. I looked at the flight schedule and couldn't believe the route. I would have to fly from Manchester to London, then on to Brussels, Zaire and Johannesburg, finally arriving at Durban. I guess that must have been the cheapest route. At this point I have to tell you that I was a naive twenty-four-year-old. I didn't follow world events and hadn't a clue about the apartheid situation in South Africa but I would experience it at first hand.

Mick Miller

My 1st publicity photo

I took my flights and finally arrived in Johannesburg. I felt like Phileas Fogg after his eighty days around the world. Unfortunately, the trip was not without casualties. You see, I had decided to wear an old pair of patent leather "stage boots." They were lined with soft foam lining, very comfortable when stood on stage for an hour, but not such a good idea for the long plane journey. By the time I was on the final leg of the journey my feet were getting soggy. In fact, as I walked down the aisle to go to the toilet, I could feel a squelching from inside the shoes. I was very aware of the smell that was emitting from them.

I cleared customs and wheeled my luggage out into "arrivals". As soon as I reached the public area an excitable woman greeted me. "Are you Mick Miller, Michael Lawton?" I introduced myself and she grabbed me, "Quickly" she said, "we only have four minutes". I thought we must have been under nuclear attack. It turned out that I was being put on the internal flight to Durban and had only four minutes to catch it. We made it and I settled into my seat. I was sat next to a very smart businessman. Bear in mind I had been travelling for a long time and was looking a bit worse for wear. He looked at me, sniffed and casually took out a small aftershave spray. He squirted himself twice and then pressed it once more. This time it was pointing at my feet. I couldn't believe it but I didn't complain. After all, my feet were getting smellier and I was glad of the fresh smell.

The local agent, Peter Hubbard, met me at Durban. He was a small man, only about five feet four inches, but he was also about four feet six inches round! He reminded me of "The Fat Controller". He took me to "The Beach Hotel" where I checked in to my eighth floor room. It was basic, but comfortable. There was no TV in South Africa in those days but there was a radio in the room. All I wanted to do was run a bath and have a long soak. I went into the bathroom to run it. Whilst it was running I stripped off and removed the shoes. The smell was horrendous. I made the decision there and then to throw them away.

The bath was ready and I couldn't wait to get in. My feet were in a terrible state, all white and wrinkled. You'd have thought that they'd been in water for about nine weeks! I entered the bathroom and stopped in my tracks. There, between the bath and me was the biggest cockroach I had ever seen. It had huge antennae and wings. In fact it looked like the size of a Cessna two-seater plane to me. There was only one thing to do, stamp on it, but I had just thrown the shoes away. So, I returned to the bin, retrieved the shoes and crept back into the bathroom like an SAS soldier. What a sight, a naked man in smelly patent leather shoes, jumping up and down trying to kill a cockroach. Mission accomplished I finally got my bath.

The night was still young, so after my bath I decided to go out for a breath of fresh air. It was so hot and I just couldn't settle in my room. I crossed the road and walked along the promenade. In the distance I could hear chanting and what sounded like drumming. The area was deserted and I began to feel uneasy. The noise was getting closer and I could now see what was causing it. Making their way up the road were about ten Zulu warriors. They carried on chanting and banging their shields with their spears. They were getting closer and I was getting worried. I speeded up and ran in the opposite direction. I ran across the road and into a small bar. I ordered a beer and the barman asked if I was OK. I was shaking as I told him about the Zulu warriors who had chased me up the street. He started to laugh: in fact he nearly fell on the floor laughing. I asked what was so funny and he explained about the tribal dancing competition in the stadium just down the road. I had been in no danger at all: they were just having a good time and practising their dances in the street. I felt like a right prat.

The next day I was due to work in the hotel's cabaret room. So, during the afternoon, I had to go in for the "band call" and rehearse the show. I was pleased to find that most of the band and cast were British, so I felt at home. This soon turned out to be a false sense of security because that evening was one of the hardest of my career. Not quite as bad as that night with Jimmy Jones, but very nearly. The audience were mainly white South Africans and weren't too keen on a balding scouse comic. I began to wonder if I had done the right thing in going out there for three months.

Chapter 6

South Africa and Noddy

I found myself sitting alone in my hotel room in Durban, South Africa, feeling very down. I was two weeks into my three-month contract and maybe I should have done a bit more research about this country before I took the work. I didn't know about the apartheid system. I was just a failed footballer who was trying to make a living doing comedy. I'm a "people person" and I enjoy chatting to everyone I meet, but here, I wasn't allowed to mix with the local black population. I couldn't chat to the person who served my breakfast and ask them how they were etc. This was totally alien to me and, as each day went by, I grew more and more disillusioned working there. To say that the shows were going badly for me was an understatement and, because of that, none of the other acts wanted to be associated with me. I felt very alone and very lonely.

It was at this point that I opened my bottle of duty free gin. There was no TV, so I turned on the small short-wave radio that I had brought with me and tuned into the BBC World service. You can imagine how alone I felt in this strange country, with just a crackling radio and a bottle of gin for company. To make it worse it was "Children's Hour" and as I poured my gin, the presenter introduced "The Noddy Show." Well, that was nearly the straw that broke the camel's back! I took a large swig of gin and sat back to be entertained by Noddy! My glass was soon empty and, just as the presenter said, "Hello children, what does Noddy do today? He wakes up and goes to the bathroom for a wash. Noddy fills the sink with water" I was pouring gin into my glass. The pouring gin sounded like a sound effect and made me smile and I said out loud, "Oh, Noddy's got a big sink!" as I poured a very large gin. As the story went on I found myself laughing for the first time in what seemed like ages. As Noddy made his breakfast, in my mind the presenter became a raging alcoholic who hated kids. I just imagined him in the studio making the story up and drinking his way through it. All I could think of was this man getting very drunk as he told the story. To me, sat alone in my room, this was funny. So I picked up my notepad and wrote it down. It took a while, because by now, I was quite tipsy, but it turned out to be the best thing that I have ever done in my career, because that routine became the mainstay of my act and opened so many doors for me.

The next morning when I awoke, the notepad was still on my bedside table. I read what I had written and it was still funny, so I started to refine it. I felt very positive and for the first time was looking forward to that night's gig. Something had changed inside me and I just felt good on stage. I wanted to do my Noddy routine but it wasn't anywhere like ready to be performed. I think that the adrenalin must have kicked in, because I gave the best performance I had given in ages. The audience lapped it up and I felt that I'd turned a corner. All of a sudden, the other acts decided to talk to me, but it was too late by then. They didn't want to know me when I wasn't doing well, so with just a week left in Durban, I couldn't be bothered with them. I don't like two-faced people.

Because I was due to move on down to Cape Town, a new comedian arrived to work the Durban area. It turned out to be my good friend, Stu Francis. We met up and had a game of golf, followed by some surfing etc. That night, the other new acts in town came to the show. My confidence was now back where it should have been and I had a great gig. After the show, Tony Christie introduced himself to me. He was one of the new acts and it made a pleasant change to be with nice people. Tony and I became close friends and, later on, I did several tours with him as his support act.

The next act to arrive was a ventriloquist called Neville King. He was an amazing act and he later became a mentor to me. I owe a lot to this man, but I will come back to him later in this book.

All too soon I had to leave for Cape Town. The last week in Durban had been fantastic, but all good things must come to an end. I had met people who would be friends for life and others that I wouldn't cross the road to see. So I packed my bags and headed off to the airport.

Cape Town was very different to Durban. It was altogether more English and didn't feel as alien to me. I settled into my hotel and looked at things to do on my nights off. A local football team called Hellenic was playing at home, so that looked like a good night out to me. The day came and I made my way to the ground. There was a great atmosphere as I went in. I bought a match day programme, and looked at the team selection. Amazingly, they had a player called Ronnie Wilson, which was the same name as a full back at Port Vale when I was there. As the teams came out I looked for him. Could it be the same man? The game started, but this Ronnie Wilson had long hair, tied back with a headband. The "Port Vale" Ronnie Wilson was bald, but the style of play was very familiar. Could it be a wig? The funny thing was that since my Port Vale days, my flowing locks had receded and, if this was the same man, his had done the opposite.

The next night I was working at The Carlton Hotel and the football team had come in to see the English cabaret. After the show Ronnie came up to me at the bar and complimented me on my act. He looked me up and down and said, "I'm sure I know you." Well I certainly knew him, but not his long hair! Had the South African sunshine done something miraculous, or was he just wearing a wig? I think it was the latter. I decided to have some fun with him and told him that he had probably seen me on TV, even though I had never been on TV. He was adamant that he knew me from somewhere and that it wasn't from TV. I had him going for over an hour when his wife arrived and immediately said, "Oh my God, it's Micky Lawton, the Port Vale goalie!" Ronnie was gobsmacked and said, "You've lost your hair!" I replied, "And you've obviously found some!" He laughed and introduced me to the rest of the team. They were a great bunch and invited me to train with them, an offer I took up. When I got there I was surprised to see a familiar face. Albert Hammond, who had just been in the charts with, "It Never Rains in Southern California" was a big star and here was I training with him. He went on to have major success in the music world, but he was just a normal, everyday type of bloke who was just one of the lads.

From there I was invited to players' houses for barbecues and was made so welcome that I was sad to leave when my three week stint came to an end. But I had to go and was on the flight back up to Durban. My next three weeks would be at The Goodison Hotel in a small cocktail lounge. I had to do a 7.00pm cocktail hour show! I know that sounds bizarre, but it's what I had to do. The room was very small and only held about eighty people. It was a bit off the beaten track and apparently twenty-five people would be a good audience for them.

Sure enough, my first night had about that many in, but after the show I got talking to some Scouse lads at the bar. They were members of the crew of "The Pendenis Castle", a ship that was in port for several days. They had really enjoyed the gig and said that they would spread the word on the ship and come back the next night. True to their word they came back with lots of friends and the room was full. The owner was amazed and seemed to think I was obviously some kind of star back in the UK. For four nights the lads from the ship filled the room and the owner was making a fortune. I was worried what would happen when the ship sailed, but I needn't have bothered, because word had got around that you had to get there early to see my show, so the room was full every night from then on. I was pleased that everything had gone well and that in my last wage packet there was a "little extra" for doing so well.

I had been in South Africa for nine weeks and I'd grown to love the country. I hated the way they treated "the blacks" but it was a stunning place to be. I had been on safaris and seen lions being fed by dropping a dead cow off the back of a truck. I had played golf on some of the world's greatest golf courses. I had surfed and swam at the most amazing beaches and met some great people. But I never returned there until the apartheid regime had gone. I now visit on cruise ships and it is a wonderful country.

I had three more weeks to do in Africa and flew up to Rhodesia, which is now Zimbabwe. It was hot and sticky when I came out of the airport and I had been told that someone who would take me to my digs would meet me. As I looked around I saw this small scruffy man with a clubfoot and a hump. I remember thinking, "I hope it's not him." In fact, I thought he was a beggar! Sure enough, he came up to me and said, "Mick Miller?" I said, "Yes" and he introduced himself as, "Curry Le Strange," the agent who had booked me. I know you think that I have made up that name, but I haven't. He was actually called Curry Le Strange!

He led me to a beat-up old Datsun car and drove me to the club where I would be working. On top of the club was a tatty flat, which was to be my home for the next three weeks. It was like something you might find in Beirut, but that is where I had to live. At least it was very handy for work.

The club was full of expats, and the gigs were OK. But on my days off I did some extra gigs for the local Rotary and Round Table clubs. They paid me in Rhodesian money and, being a bit naïve, I didn't realise that you couldn't take the money out of the country. So on my last day at the club I gathered all the waiters together and split the money between them. They were over the moon. Nobody had ever done this before and they were so grateful as they didn't earn much. It wasn't until I got home that I found out that the normal thing to do was buy gold and bring it home to sell. Still, it was nice to be able to help those waiters out.

I do remember that wrestling was very big in Rhodesia at that time and many of the big-name wrestling stars from the UK were working out there. Some of them came to see my show and I got to know them. People like "Rollerball Roco," "The Royal Brothers" and "Tony Banger Walsh" regularly worked over there. These guys were big stars in the UK and here was I chatting to them at the bar.

Well, being young and fit, I had an idea for a comedy routine. I thought that it would be funny to do a mime about wrestling. I ran it past the guys and they agreed to help me plan it. The final part involved me doing a back flip and landing flat on my back. I worked on it for ages and perfected it. I did this routine for many years, but finally gave it up after doing it on "Today with Des & Mel." I realised I was getting older and it hurt! But funnily enough, I got a tweet from one of today's big wrestling stars, William Regal, to say how much he enjoyed that routine. It turns out that he is a big fan and regularly sings my praises on Twitter.

Finally, my three-month culture shock was over and I returned to the UK. I was a lot more tanned and also a lot more aware of the politics of Africa. But at least I could now put "International Comedian" on my publicity! I was 24-years old and had grown up a lot during my African adventure. I had a new-found confidence in my ability to make people laugh and I knew that I was meant to do this. I was ready for bigger and better things back in the UK.

Chapter 7

Clubs and TV

When I got home from Rhodesia I called my manager, Stuart Littlewood to see where I would be working over the next few months. I expected him to give me a few dates here and there, but to my surprise he told me that my diary was full for the next year. I had never been in this position in my life. I used to worry how I was going to pay the rent and here I was, knowing where I would be working on a Tuesday ten months ahead!

This was 1974 and club land was buzzing. Cabaret clubs were the places to go. They would be open every night and the early week shows would have cheaper admission fees, so they were accessible to everyone. This was great for acts like me, as we got to work all week. The money was good and the food was served in a basket.

For those of you who don't know, these clubs used to present stars like Shirley Bassey, Tom Jones, The Stylistics, Neil Sedaka and Johnny Mathis. Of course, they all needed support acts, and I was now one of those support acts. This was a different world to me, I mean, I'm quite shy offstage and here I am mixing with major stars. One of the first clubs I worked was "Caesar's Palace" in Luton. I was booked to support Shirley Bassey and was quite nervous, I mean, what would I say to her. I needn't have worried because I never met her. I was on at 9.00pm and she was on at 10.30pm. She arrived whilst I was on stage and didn't leave her dressing room until she was about to go on stage. But my main memory of this gig was a lesson that I learned from the club's manager. He was a guy who is a legend within showbiz and is a friend to the stars, George Savva.

It was my first show for him and I was told to do forty minutes. So, I went on stage to do my act. The club was great and so was the audience. I was enjoying myself and wanted to give a good performance. I was on for forty-five minutes and got a standing ovation. As I came off stage and headed back to my dressing room, George Savva was heading towards me. I looked at him, expecting him to say how well I'd done, but no. He slapped me on the back of my head and said, "You've just cost me a grand!" I looked blank, I didn't understand. He then explained that the extra five minutes that I had done was time that the audience should have been spending money at the bar. He said that they should have taken about a thousand pounds in those five minutes. I apologised and promised not to do it again. I realised that this was the business side of show business and that is what paid my wages. It was a valuable lesson and I've never forgotten it. So when I was asked to do forty minutes the following week at the "Sheffield Fiesta", I made damn sure I didn't overrun. However, when I came off stage, the manager sent me back on to do five more minutes because he wanted his money's worth out of me! I suppose that's the difference between north and south.

I got on really well with the band at the Sheffield Fiesta and on the Saturday afternoon I joined them for a drink. Apparently one of them wanted to celebrate the fact that his wife was pregnant, so a drink was in order. We couldn't drink too much as we were working that night. So on the way back from the pub he wanted to call into "Mothercare" to pick up some things for the baby. He had a list of stuff to get from his wife. We followed him around the shop as he loaded up the trolley with everything you could possibly need for a baby. There was a car seat, a potty, packs of nappies and the trolley was piled high. We headed to the checkouts, which were absolutely packed. As we started to queue, he said that he had forgotten to get some babies' bottles and would I keep the place in the queue whilst he went to get them. I thought no more about it until I realised that I was next to the till. I looked around behind me, but there was no sign of him. Then I looked forward and then I saw all the guys stood outside at the window. They were all laughing and pulling faces at me. They had totally set me up. Here I was with a trolley full of baby items that I didn't want and I was next in line to pay. I had to say to the woman at the till that I didn't want any of the stuff and sheepishly ran out of the shop to some strange looks and raucous laughter from outside. They had set me up and I totally fell for it. Somehow, I think that they may have done this wind-up before on other unsuspecting support acts.

I was now getting into the swing of being the support act and turned up at "Stockton Fiesta Club" to work with Frankie Vaughan who was from Liverpool and was now a big star with many hit records under his belt. In fact he was a bit of a hero to me. As usual, he hadn't arrived when I went on to do my forty minutes. I did well and came off stage sweating and knackered due to the heat of the lights. As I stood there, I heard a knock at the door, so I opened it. To my surprise, there stood Frankie Vaughan and his wife. They stepped inside and Frankie said, "Could you get me a coffee please," so I went and made him a coffee and took it to his dressing room. He thanked me and I left the room. It was the first time I had actually met a big star and I had to make him a coffee!

Soon after, I was in my dressing room when there was a knock on the door. It was the manager and he said, "Frankie Vaughan wants to say hello and thank you for being the support act." With that, in walked Frankie. We looked at each other and he said, "You're the support act? I'm so sorry, I didn't realise." He had thought I was the stage doorman and that is why he had asked for a coffee. He did say that he thought it odd that I was sweating so much, but now it all made sense. He kept apologising, but I saw the funny side of it. He asked me why I didn't tell him to get his own coffee and I said, "Well, my mother always brought me up to be polite and if Frankie Vaughan asks for a coffee, I'll make Frankie Vaughan a coffee."

A man called Les Cox came to see me work at Caesar's Palace in Luton. It was now 1975 and he was the producer of the TV talent show, "New Faces." This man had the ability to turn people into stars and he liked my act. After the show, he came to see me in my dressing room and told me that he wanted me on the show. True to his word, he contacted Stuart Littlewood and three weeks later I was on the TV in front of millions of viewers. This was prime time television and doing this show could catapult you into the big league.

I remember watching the other acts rehearse and thinking that the act to beat was "Sheer Elegance", a very slick vocal group. All I could do was give it my all and hope for the best. The panel that night consisted of Tony Hatch, Mickie Most and Clifford Davis. None of them liked comedy so I was shitting myself. I had three minutes to impress them so I did my now tried and tested "Noddy" routine. The audience loved it, but better still, the panel were very positive as well.

Then, "Sheer Elegance" took to the stage and I have to say they were excellent. I thought they would win, but during their routine, one of them made a mistake whilst dancing and knocked their mic stand over. The panel jumped on that mistake and lo and behold, I won the heat and went on to an "All Winners" show, where I didn't do so well. It was won by a vocal group called "Ofanchi" who went on to do very well in the main final.

The club circuit was very good to me. It allowed me to develop my act and the best way to improve is to work as much as possible. I have very fond memories of those days and have so many stories about them. I was living in Liverpool at the time and Liverpool produced so many great comedians. We all knew each other and would often go to see each other when we had nights off. There were so many characters around and some of them went on to be household names. My friends at that time were people like Les Dennis, Stan Boardman and many others.

As well as those who went on to national stardom, others became very well-known on the club circuit and many of them were hilariously funny. Pete Price is now a popular radio presenter, but back then he was working the club circuit as a comedian. Pete was openly gay and was very camp onstage. He used to wear a suit made up of cloth, printed to look like a newspaper. He would walk on and his opening line was, "don't you see some queer things in the newspapers!" He would often pick on a good-looking woman in the front row and compliment her on her looks. Then he would ask if she had any brothers! Nobody could take offence at him as he was so likeable.

Jackie Hamilton was the Liverpool comedian's comedian. He was admired by everyone, but never became a big name outside Liverpool. He died in 2003 and it was a very sad day for comedians everywhere. It would be fair to say that he liked a drink and there are many stories about him. One time he turned up at a club and asked for his money. When the concert secretary refused, he asked why. The answer was simple, "You haven't been on yet!" Jackie looked confused and replied, "Well I've been on somewhere tonight."

As an Equity member, Jackie used to do quite a bit of TV and film work. He was what is now known as a "Background Artiste" or "Extra," and when Barbra Streisand came to Liverpool to film scenes for "Yentl" Jackie was first in the queue to be a Jewish immigrant on the ship taking them to America. The Mersey Ferry was to be this ship for the film. Jackie was wrapped in a blanket looking poor and cold. Barbra sang a haunting song and it was all very emotional. As she started to sing, you could cut the atmosphere with a knife, she was so good. But halfway through the song, the call, "Cut" was shouted. Everything was reset and she started again. This time she had only sang for a short while before "Cut" was called again. After another couple of takes, Jackie, dressed as the Jewish immigrant shouted, "Come on Babs, get it right, I've got to be at Walton Labour Club at half past eight!" I know that a lot of people laughed, but I don't know what Ms Streisand thought.

Liverpool had several big theatre clubs: "The Wooky Hollow", "The Shakespeare", "Allinsons" and "The Hamilton" in Birkenhead were all very popular and, again, I would be booked to do a week at each of them. In fact sometimes I would work at two of them in one night. Pete Price was the resident compère at The Shakespeare and one night I was working there with "Peters & Lee." Their big hit, "Welcome Home" had been number one in the charts and the club had sold out for the week. Lennie Peters was totally blind and had to be guided on and off stage. Well, after the band call in the afternoon, Diane Lee asked me if I could guide Lennie to the Gents. So, I took his arm and led the way. We were talking about the football as I opened the door and led him to the urinals. "It's straight in front of you Lennie" I said as I turned around and switched the light on. As he heard the click of the switch, he just said, "Prat!" I felt awful: I had just turned the lights on for a blind man. Lennie then laughed, he had just found it funny.

I was lucky enough to work with Tommy Cooper at the Wooky Hollow. The stage was like something out of "Saturday Night Fever", but this was well before that film came out. It was made up of glass panels with coloured lights under each pane of glass. It looked great and was the big feature of the club as it lowered and became the dance floor. Tommy Cooper arrived and set up all of his props. He used to do a routine that involved eggs, the finale of which was throwing an egg into the air and supposedly catching it on a plate. However, the egg that he threw up was a fake, made of marble and would smash the plate and it got a big laugh. So during the show he performed this routine, but nobody had thought about the marble egg hitting the glass floor. Of course it just smashed the glass panel. The next night, I was about to go on stage, when the stage manager told me that they hadn't been able to get it repaired and had just put some coloured lighting gel in its place to disguise it. He told me to stay away from the blue square, which wasn't a problem. The next night, the same thing happened and by the end of the week I couldn't stand on the blue, yellow, red, green, purple or orange panels. I hate to think how much that was going to cost the club to repair, but they must have made a fortune that week as Tommy was one of the biggest names in the business.

I would go on to work with Tommy Cooper many more times in my career and I have to say he was one of my all-time favourites. I just had to look at his props set up on stage and I would start laughing. In my opinion, he was a genius.

Not many of these type of clubs survived the recession of the late 1970's and early 80's, but a few did. Bob Potter's Lakeside Club near Camberley did survive and now hosts the big darts tournaments. Bob was a stickler about his rules and the one that he enforced the most was that no artiste was allowed out into the public areas of the club. He, quite rightly, thought that when people pay to see you perform, you should remain slightly out of touch, otherwise the showbiz glamour would be tainted. To maintain his stance, he provided comfortable dressing rooms and a private backstage bar. You could order food, play pool and just relax there. If you had family or guests at the show, they could come there to meet you. I was fine with this and used to look forward to working there. But some acts didn't like this rule and would try sneaking out into the main room. In fact one of The Stylistics, who were a black American group, was caught sneaking into the club. Bob stopped him and explained that he wasn't allowed to go there. Unfortunately, it was taken the wrong way. He thought that he was back in the deep south of America and it was because of his skin colour. There was very nearly an international incident until Bob explained his rule properly and pointed to me over in the corner. I'll never forget his words, "Even that bald bastard isn't allowed out there!" I just sat there and shrugged my shoulders. To this day I am still friends with Bob Potter and often call in to see him if I'm passing.

I could go on and on about these days. There are so many stories to tell so one day I might write another book just about the clubs. I was doing well and earning a few bob and with that came the nice cars and the good living. I bought a Ford Cortina 2000E which was very very quick. It was my pride and joy and one night when I was working at the

Wooky Hollow, the owner, Terry Philips, invited me to their staff party. He suggested that I take my car home and get a taxi back, as if I left it there overnight, it would get nicked. I didn't want to lose it, so I drove it home and parked up. The party was great and when I left, it was snowing. As my taxi pulled up to the house, I was shocked to see a car shaped piece of tarmac in the snow where my car had been parked. You've guessed it, it had been nicked from outside the house! The next day, the Police called me to say that they had found it in one of the rougher areas of the city and I could pick it up from there. Luckily it wasn't damaged, but I was upset that some scrote had been driving it and sold it shortly afterwards.

At this point, I was still living at my parents' house, which was great for me as my mum looked after me, did my washing and made my meals. I had cash in my pocket and was relishing the single lifestyle. The only downside was that I couldn't take girls home for "liaisons." The time had come for me to get a flat, so I rented one in Birkenhead. It was great if I pulled a girl at Hamilton's Club as it was just around the corner. But I still spent loads of time living in Wavertree at my parents. The flat was just for "fun."

Things were going well and I was enjoying my life, but something was bothering me. Stuart Littlewood's office was growing and eventually merged with another big agency, "Kennedy Street Artistes." Together, they now looked after the likes of 10cc and Tony Christie, as well as Cannon & Ball and Stu Francis. I started to worry that with a set of clients like that I might be pushed to one side. I still don't know if that would have happened, because I decided to leave them and go to a Liverpool based agent called Ricky McCabe.

Ricky's office was in the famous Liver Building and he was looking after a lot of the Liverpool acts. I felt that I had made the right decision and waited for the work to roll in. I wasn't disappointed, as he managed to get me loads of gigs. I was very busy and I was still very ambitious.

It was 1979 and I used to play football for the local "Showbiz Eleven" team. One of the team was a local play writer called Alan Bleasdale. He was riding high on his TV successes and he always seemed to have something on the go.

One night, after a charity match, Alan pulled me to one side in the dressing room. He explained that he had written a new play, which was about to be filmed by the BBC. He explained that there was a part in it that would suit me down to the ground and would I be interested in it. I didn't need asking twice. His reputation was immense and this could be very good for me. The deal was done and I was contracted to do the play. It was called "Scully's New Year's Eve" and I was to play the role of Joey. John Junkin was to play my father and Avis Bunnage my mother. Filming was to be at BBC's Pebble Mill studios in Birmingham and would take four weeks.

I arrived at the studio for the first day and met the cast. We were called to the office in turn to collect our "expenses." Now, being new to this acting business, I didn't know about the expenses system for actors. I was given about £400 in cash to cover food and accommodation for the filming period. I immediately rang the local Holiday Inn Hotel and booked in for the month. The cost was approximately £400, so I was happy. The other cast members had all booked rooms in peoples' houses. I couldn't believe it, but that's how they earned extra money. They treated "expenses" as part of the wage and tried not to spend it, but I was happy in my comfortable hotel.

The play aired on BBC1 on a Monday night and all my family and friends were tuned in, but sadly my Uncle Norman had died a few days earlier. My father was estranged from his family, and didn't see his brother but thought that he should go to the funeral, which was on the day after the play went out. He asked me to go with him for a bit of support.

We arrived at Allerton Crematorium and sat at the back. The hearse arrived and the coffin was brought in. The service started and we listened carefully as the vicar sang the praises of, "ERIC." We looked at each other as it dawned on us that we were at the wrong funeral. You see Allerton Crematorium has two chapels and on busy days they are both holding funerals at the same time. We had to sneak out of Eric's funeral and run around to the other chapel for Uncle Norman's, so we managed to catch the start of Eric's and the end of Norman's!

Scouse wit knows no boundaries and, as I was standing outside the chapel, one of the funeral directors recognised me from the play that had been on TV the previous night. The climax of the play was when I found a dead body and this guy leaned over to me and said, "That was quick, you only found the body at 11.00pm last night!" It could have been a bit insensitive, but as I didn't really know Uncle Norman, I found it amusing.

Throughout 1980, I worked around the Liverpool club circuit and came across some great characters that were involved in that scene. I will never forget Ernie Mack, who was an agent and also owned "The Montrose Club" and "The McGull Country Club". He would always fight to get the best deal and had the worst wig in the world. He was one of those people who talked out of the corner of his mouth, so when the phone rang on this particular day, I knew instantly who was on the other end. Ernie was hosting The "Arthur Askey Showbiz Awards" and he was calling to let me know that due to my hard work and audience reaction, along with voting from the club owners, I had won "Comedian of The Year." All I had to do was turn up at his club and do half an hour for free, then pick up my award. I checked my diary and told him that I was already working elsewhere on this date, so it would be difficult for me to get there and perform. Without batting an eyelid, Ernie just said, "Oh, that's OK, we'll give it so someone else!" You can imagine what that did to my ego.

I did work at The McGull for Ernie, when he persuaded me to work cheap as the support for Lena Zavaroni, who had had a big hit with, "Ma, He's Making Eyes At Me." The club was packed and, after my act, Bill Dean, who went on to play Harry Cross in Brookside, came up to me. At that time he was just getting into acting, but had been a very traditional comedian. I went to shake his hand, but he just looked at me and said, "I'm disgusted with you, you said, Fart, on stage." I couldn't believe what he was saying and quick as a flash, I said, "Well you said, F★★K in the film, Scum." He didn't even try to reply to that and just walked away.

The following year, I was actually awarded the Arthur Askey Showbiz Award and was very proud to have it presented to me by Ken Dodd. I still have that trophy, although it isn't on my mantelpiece.

Chapter 8

Summer Season and "The Comedians" Beckon

Back to 1977 and Ricky McCabe decided to have a go at producing a "Seaside Summer Show" and I was part of his plans. It felt like I was now on the road to bigger success, as summer seasons were what all the big names did at that time. The show was to star "Our Kid," the Liverpool band that had won New Faces. Other acts on the bill included Monica Rose, who was famous as Hughie Green's sidekick on his TV game show and Cardew "The Cad" Robinson. To this day I still don't know what he did! I think he was supposed to be a comedian, but he didn't get many laughs.

I was very proud to be part of a summer season show and arrived at The "Winter Gardens" in Morecambe ready for the experience. I was expecting glamour in a beautiful traditional British theatre. What I got was a crumbling auditorium and a damp dressing room. When I looked up at the ceiling in the theatre, there was a net protecting the audience from the bits of plaster that regularly fell off. To say that the theatre was in disrepair would be unfair: it was actually a shit hole!

I didn't have much in common with the rest of the cast, so after the shows I would head on down to a cabaret venue called "The Battery", where Jim Bowen was performing for the summer. Jim was already a big success on the TV show, "The Comedians" and we hit it off straight away. I would have a drink with him and then go on to the local nightclub, "The Morecambe Bowl," which was also a cabaret venue that I had worked in regularly in the past. I had become a party animal who slept all day and partied all night.

Unbeknown to me, the theatre manager, Keith West, really liked my act, and had contacted Blackpool legend, Peter Webster, who had moved on from being a children's entertainer to being a theatre impresario. Peter put summer shows on at both the Central and South Pier theatres in Blackpool and was a major player in the Blackpool showbiz community.

Neville King

Without me knowing, Peter came to see the show. The first thing I knew about it was through a phone call at the end of the season from an agency called "Forrester George." Peter used them to book all the artistes for his summer shows and had told them he wanted me. It was a no-brainer. Six months in a Blackpool show was just too good to turn down. So I accepted and was happy to know that I had so much work in the diary, but I had the long winter months to survive.

Ricky McCabe came up with work for me, but most of it was in the Liverpool area. Sure, it was easy work, but I wanted to keep travelling. I didn't want to get stuck in a rut just working in Liverpool. This was preying on my mind through the winter, but I had agreed to work for him for a contracted period of time, but would leave him after the Blackpool season to work for Forrester George.

My stint in Blackpool was nearly six months long and I had booked into a small hotel near the South Pier for the duration. Comedy group, "Candlewick Green", headlined the show and the other acts were Russ Stevens (magician) and the ventriloquist that I had met in South Africa, Neville King. We did two shows a night at 6.10 and 8.40 for six nights and had Sundays off.

Russ Stevens was quite young at the time and was still perfecting his act. He was very good though and produced two poodles from what appeared to be nowhere. Unfortunately, they were also quite young and didn't have great bladder control, so as soon as they appeared from their hiding place they would head straight to the curtain and pee on them. The audience always laughed, but the stage manager wasn't too happy about it.

For his big finish, he produced a white cockatoo that was supposed to hop onto a perch to rapturous applause. It was a beautiful-looking bird, but I had got to know it backstage. It had a plume of feathers on its head which stood up if it was angry and you wouldn't want to know it when it was angry! One night, instead of hopping on to its perch, it flew off into the theatre. We had no option other than to carry on with the show. As I walked on to the stage, I put my arm out towards Russ and said, "Ladies and gentlemen, the fantastic Russ Stevens." At this point, the cockatoo decided to land on my arm, so I moved to the side of the stage to allow Russ to get the bird, but it was having none of it. It repositioned itself on my other shoulder and just looked at me whilst the yellow plume rose up. It was really pissed off! So, being a coward and not wanting to antagonise it any more, I did my twelve-minute spot with a cockatoo on my shoulder. I can honestly say that I have never done that since.

Something else that I have never done since that season is use hair crimpers! We were a couple of weeks into the shows and everyone was getting to know each other. These were the days when every show had a team of dancers and our team was always up for a laugh. One of the girls had bought the very latest gadget – hair crimpers and had brought them in to the theatre. The girls thought it would be funny to crimp my hair for a bit of fun. They told me that the crimps would just brush out so, like a fool, I agreed. It looked hilarious and we all had a good laugh and took some photos. It was now time to get ready for the show, so I went back to my dressing room and washed my hair. To my horror, my hair frizzed out like an afro! I desperately tried to smooth it down, but the more I tried, the worse it got. I had to go on stage for the next few nights with frizzy hair: I looked like the Sphinx!

But it was Neville King who impressed me. He was so polished as a performer. He was always immaculately dressed and such a confident person. I hadn't seen him since South Africa, but he had become a regular on TV shows and was now quite well known. His main dummy was an old man, simply known as Grandad, who was quite grumpy and rude on stage, but if he ever got him out at a party, he swore like a trooper!

I would watch Neville's act night after night, he was that good. He was quite a bit older than me, but he took me under his wing. If he was invited to a party he made sure that I was invited too. I was keen to improve as a comedian and started chatting to Neville about some of my ideas. He helped me work on my timing and even where to stand on a stage and how to work an audience. These are skills that you take you years to perfect but make a big difference when performing. Neville taught me everything he knew about it over the six months in Blackpool and I will never forget him for that.

This was 1978 and Blackpool was the place to be. There were seven theatres running summer shows with people like Les Dawson and The Bachelors as the headline acts. So after the shows, many of us would meet up in "The Viking Hotel" where the owner, Eric Slack, had a "Late Bar" for the acts that were working on the shows. If we weren't there, we would be at "The Galleon" which was frequented by most of the musicians in the town. I don't think I ever went to bed before sunrise.

There was one memorable night when I didn't go out after the show. Neville had to return home to Nottinghamshire and had asked me to go with him. I agreed and, as we walked to his car, he handed me the keys and said, "You're driving." So like a mug, I drove whilst he slept. When we arrived at his cottage, he invited me in and showed me through to my room. To get there we had to pass his office/workshop and he opened the door to show me his works in progress. There were heads with eyes hanging out and a Blackpool-type landlady with a fag hanging out of her mouth. As we walked to my room, there were stuffed animals on shelves, which included a mongoose catching a snake. It was all quite creepy in the dark.

As I put my bags in the room, Neville announced that he was going out as he was meeting a lady friend. I was left alone in the house and it was creaking the way that old houses do. I needed to go to the toilet, so I went down the corridor, past the office where the heads looked at me through the open door, past the mongoose and snake and made it safely to the toilet. Then I did the route back to the bedroom. As I lay in bed, all I could hear was the creaking and the vision of those heads kept popping into my mind. I couldn't sleep and, after about an hour, I needed to go to the toilet again, so I got dressed and made my way down the corridor. It was very creepy, so I went to the toilet and then carried on to the front door, went outside and slept in the car! I just couldn't cope with all those things looking at me. I was convinced that something would get me in the night.

When I awoke in the morning Neville was back. He asked why I was in the car and, to be honest, I felt stupid. I was 28-years-old and had been scared of some half-made puppets and stuffed animals. He never let me forget that night.

It was during this season that I started seeing a girl called Diane. Her mother was from Malta, and owned the hotel where I was stopping. Diane was the eldest of six daughters. It was quite nice having a steady relationship and she would come along to the shows and parties with me. I was getting used to having her around and decided to stop on throughout the winter. I had made lots of friends over those six months and enjoyed being in Blackpool, but I was ready for a short break.

Ricky McCabe was due to go away for a month, so he sent me a contract with some bookings for me. The first show was at a rugby club in South Wales at 12.00 on the Sunday lunchtime after I had finished the Blackpool season on the Saturday night. A gig in Oxford followed this on the Sunday night, then Torquay and Weymouth. I immediately rang him and told him that I hadn't agreed to do these gigs because I wanted a week off. He wasn't very happy and said that I would have to do them as he had agreed them with another agent called John Mills, who was based in Bristol. Ricky refused to call him to get me out of the work. So, I got hold of John Mills' number and called him myself. I explained that I hadn't agreed to do these gigs and wouldn't be doing them. John was livid and, after calling me some choice names, he threatened to take me to court, take me to the Agents' Association and take me to the cleaners! But I simply pointed out that on the contract, it clearly stated that all gigs would be within a thirty-mile radius of Bristol and if he tried to take any action against me, due to the mileage involved, I would take him to the Department of Transport! This story flew around the business and Eddie Large has dined out on it for years. I never did do those gigs and, soon after, I left Ricky's office and signed to Forrester George.

After my short break, it was back to work, but I had made the decision to live in Blackpool. It was a great place to be and I was still with Diane. The parties continued and I was living the life I wanted.

During that winter, Diane's mother bought a restaurant on Central Drive in Blackpool. It had six flats above it and it seemed to be sensible to rent one. Her sisters occupied the other flats and I never thought that there would be a problem with that. However, I was sadly mistaken. Don't get me wrong, I got along with all of them, but sisters being sisters, they all got involved in each other's business and relationships. It was a case of, if you kicked one, they all limped! I have to say that I never did kick one, but you know what I'm saying.

I was happy just living with Diane, but her sisters had other ideas. They seemed to like me and wanted us to get married. You can imagine five strong-minded sisters and their mother all dropping large hints about marriage. So, eventually, for a quiet life I decided to go with the flow. My single days were numbered and deep down, I knew it wasn't the right thing to do.

All too soon, the big day arrived and there I was stood at the church thinking, "Oh shit, I've dropped a bollock here." I really didn't want to go through with it. It was nothing to do with Diane, it was just that I had realised that I wasn't cut out for marriage. I looked around at all the guests: Les Dennis was there with his first wife as was Stevie Faye from The Comedians. There was even a photographer from The Daily Mirror, so I gritted my teeth and went through with it.

People often ask me what my marriage was like and to be honest it was like the old gag. It was fine, until we left the church! I don't know if it was just me feeling trapped, or that she really did change. Rules started creeping in and she started working out how long it would take me to get to and from gigs. She then checked what time I was onstage and told me what time I would be home. This wasn't what I'd signed up to and I didn't like it. It was dawning on me that I didn't really have any friends in Blackpool, just my showbiz mates who weren't there out of season. So when I found out that my old pal from Port Vale, Terry Alcock, was running Blackpool F. C. supporters' club, I immediately joined up. Let me tell you, that didn't go down well at all. If I came home late, I'd have grief from all six sisters and an irate Maltese mother.

Inevitably, my marriage was slowly going down the pan. We were living together at the flat, but I would get out as much as possible. Terry had fixed it for me to train with the players at Blackpool F.C. and I would be at the training ground by 8.30am most mornings. Then, I would be out working on the evenings and staying out in the Casino until late. I wasn't happy and I felt trapped.

Unbeknown to me, the TV producer Johnnie Hamp had been to see me during my South Pier season. He was looking for comedians for a new run of the TV series, "The Comedians". The show first aired in 1971 and ran for several years. It made stars of people like Charlie Williams, Ken Goodwin, Bernard Manning and many more. Granada TV were bringing it back and Johnnie wanted me to be a part of it along with Roy Walker and Stan Boardman.

We recorded the shows in front of a live audience and had to do a routine of short gags that could be edited into the final show. Some comedians didn't quite understand how it worked and tried to tell long, involved gags which wouldn't work with the format of the show. Su Pollard was one of the few comediennes to work on the show, but it didn't work out for her. She broke the golden rule, which was to stand relatively still on the small plinth that was the stage. She tried to move into the audience, so she was cut from the show. I think I'm right in saying that Pauline Daniels was the only woman to become a regular on the show.

There was quite a competitive atmosphere as everyone was trying to get their material into the final edit. A lot of the comedians were using "Idiot Boards", which were large pieces of card with reminders of gags on them. In those days, comedy was more about telling a joke, whereas now, it's more observational. Many different comedians would tell the same gag and we all knew every gag going. So when George Roper put his boards out early, he should have thought about Bernard Manning going on before him. Bernard took one look at them and proceeded to do everything that George was about to do.

I was very aware that there was competition to get into the final edit, so I carefully watched everyone and everything. I noticed that Jonnie Hamp seemed to use some comedians' material more than others, so I hatched a plan. If I was recording an episode with Stan Boardman, I knew that more of his stuff was likely to be used, so I noted his gag subjects. I would then hit the same subjects, as I knew it would neatly follow on from his gag in the TV edit. For example, if he did a gag about a vicar, I would do a different gag about a vicar. It seemed to work and I was used quite a lot.

I owe a lot to Jonnie Hamp, as that show was incredibly popular. We were getting 18 million viewers and it changed our lives. It meant that our fees went up and we were treated like stars. I can't believe that after all these years some of us are still working together. I will never forget what that show did for me and it was all because of Johnnie. Recently, he was awarded a Lifetime Achievement Award by the Lord Mayor of Manchester and I was honoured to attend the ceremony at Manchester Town Hall.

I am often told that The Comedians was one of the best programmes on TV and that they should bring it back. To be honest, I don't think it would work with today's younger comedians as the format was made for quick fire gags, which is not what they do. It was very much of its time and so were the jokes. It is often said that they were racist and sexist, but you have to remember that when this show went out, these jokes were the norm: we were just living in a very different world.

The shows were very successful and I was now known as a TV comedian. Out of the blue, I was offered a three-week tour with Val Doonican, which was ideal, as I would be stopping away in hotels. I thought that working to a Val Doonican audience would be easy as he was a wholesome, family-friendly Irishman, but I'd never seen him work live.

Val used to go on first, as he liked to surprise the audience. He would do five minutes and then introduce me. As he handed me the microphone, he whispered in my ear, "Good luck with these!" As I looked out from the stage, all I could see was about six rows full of nuns! What the hell do you say to make nuns laugh? I thought that this might just be a one-off nuns' night out, but it kept happening night after night. Val Doonican was obviously Top Totty for Nuns.

Other tours followed and I found myself on the road with The Drifters, which was right up my street, as I loved their music. By the time I toured with The Supremes, I was living the dream on a tour bus and away from my wife. By this time, Diana Ross was no longer with The Supremes and Mary Wilson fronted them. The first time we all met up was at the first show and I was a bit nervous. It takes a few days to get to know everyone, so sometimes you might put you foot in it.

After the show, we all boarded the bus and I joined the band in the TV lounge. They were all black and all very cool, so when one of them rolled a joint, I was half expecting it. Here I was, sat on a tour bus with a dope haze in the air and a group of black American musicians looking for a video movie to watch on the TV. Unfortunately, they chose "Gandhi", which doesn't show the British Empire in a very good light. In fact, one of the guys said, "These white Brits were bastards" so I pretended to be asleep.

The next day, I was standing in the wings by the monitor's sound engineer. Mary Wilson was onstage and was wearing the tightest one-piece Lycra costume that I've ever seen: she looked stunning. So I leaned over to the sound guy and said, "She's stunning, I definitely would…." He looked back at me and said, "Shit man, that's my mother!" So, thinking on my feet, I said, "I know, I'm just winding you up." He laughed and said, "You crack me up man, you're so funny." I think I got away with it. But I have to say what a great bunch of people they all were on that tour.

Eventually, I made the decision to end my marriage, so I moved out of our home and found a one-bedroom flat to live in. It was a bit grotty, but it was somewhere to hide away. My solicitor told me not to buy anywhere until the divorce was finalised, so this became my home for the next eighteen months. It could have been a miserable time, but I had a friend called Tony Jo, who was another comedian. He would often crash on the sofa and I daren't tell you most of the things that went on!

We were both freshly separated and playing the field. Blackpool's South Shore was our area and, even though I was reasonably well-known through my TV work, nobody bothered me. I was treated as one of the lads, which is exactly what I wanted and, if anyone ever wanted to have a go at me, Tony would step in. He was well over six-feet tall and had previously worked as a doorman.

Soon, it was time for another summer season, but this time I would be working the Pontin's circuit. It was around this time that, I started playing golf on the showbiz golf tournaments. These events raised a lot of money for charities and were always great fun to do.

Chapter 9

Showbiz and Golfing

Before I start this chapter, I should hold my hand up and tell you that I'm really crap at golf, but when you work at night, you have to fill the daytimes in and golf is one way of doing this and keeping fit. So, as there was a vibrant showbiz golfing society, I decided to give it a go.

Paul Gaskell lived on the Isle of Man and organised a lot of the celebrity tournaments. He invited me to play at Hill Valley Golf Club in Whitchurch and I was keen to get there, but the traffic was terrible and I was half an hour late. I found Paul, who looked at his watch and informed me that I was "half an hour late," and that the team that I was playing with had already gone out. I explained about the traffic and apologised profusely. I felt really bad about letting him down and said that I would just leave and go home, but Paul stopped me in my tracks, "Don't go," he said, "I need you to do ten minutes of comedy after the meal tonight."

After he had calmed down a bit, he told me not to worry too much as the "Actors" were also stuck in the traffic and they hadn't arrived either. This was a big problem, as everybody was waiting for "Gareth." I wondered who Gareth was, and it turned out to be Gareth Hunt from those coffee adverts. Apparently, he was very popular and was the star guest. Well, never one to miss a chance, I said, "Why don't you get Gareth up after dinner to do ten minutes of acting!" The look on Paul's face said it all: I thought I'd never do another showbiz golf day again. But it turned out that Paul had been stressed out over all the late arrivals and was actually very laid back. I did many more golf days for him and had an absolute ball. They were so much fun.

I made lots of new friends on that golf circuit and we often travelled together. One particular time, we were flying to Belfast during the height of the troubles. You can imagine what the security was like as we checked in at Liverpool Airport. Apart from me, there was Rick Wakeman, Lynne Perrie, Tony Christie, Willie Thorne and many more. I checked my luggage in and waited for the others. Unfortunately, Tony Christie had a problem. He was going to be performing that evening and insisted that his stage suit (in a suit bag) went as cabin luggage as he wanted to keep it crease free and immaculate. But he also had a holdall bag and the strict rule was that you were only allowed one piece of hand luggage. So, as I had no hand luggage, I offered to carry one of Tony's bags. There was no way he would trust anyone with his suit, so I carried his holdall.

As we approached the security checkpoint, everything was going well. Tony went through without any problems and I followed. But as the bag went through the scanner, the security men seemed interested in what was inside. I knew that Tony wouldn't have had anything in there that he shouldn't have, so I wasn't too worried when they asked to look inside the bag. The first thing that they pulled out was a hairdryer diffuser! It was massive and I'm sure that by pointing in the right direction you would be able to pick up Sky Sports! Four different types of hairbrushes and the biggest can of hairspray that I had ever seen followed. The look on the face of the security man was priceless as he looked at me, then at my bald head and then back at the bag, as he pulled out a large tub of hair gel and some "styling putty!"

I managed to keep a straight face as I asked them if everything was okay. I also told them to be careful when putting it all back into the bag, but it was difficult, as I could see Tony and all the gang laughing. I'm not sure if security had worked out that this wasn't actually my bag.

It was at a golf day that I first met Les Dawson. He held his own charity tournament at Lytham Golf Club, but he kept it quite low-key and just raised money for small local charities. I was quite surprised to be invited to play, but jumped at the chance to meet Les. He turned out to be everything that I'd hoped he would be and had no showbiz pretensions. He was a lovely, generous man who also happened to be very funny. He liked me and kept inviting me to different events and parties. His wife, Meg, was lovely, and they were devoted to each other, but Les did enjoy going to his Gentlemen's Club in Lytham. It was a place where he could go to just be himself and he loved it. I was one of the privileged few to be invited to join him there for a drink, but it wasn't my sort of place. It was full of old men playing cards and snooker, so I didn't become a member.

Les and I were asked to play at a corporate golf day in Stockport, so we travelled there together. The event was for professional caterers, so you can imagine how good the meal was that evening. Prize-giving time arrived and the organiser asked Les to present them, but he wasn't daft. He made an excuse and volunteered me to do it. Well, over an hour later, I was still up there presenting prizes: everyone who played that day got a prize! So by the time I got to the last one, everyone was bored sick, but my eyes lit up when the managing director of one of the big companies came on stage with a gallon bottle of whisky, thanked me for presenting the prizes and gave it to me.

I could see Les looking at this huge bottle of whisky, which was his drink of choice, and I knew he wasn't going to give up on it easily. By the time I got back to the table, he had it all worked out, "I know what we can do with that," he said. "We should both sign the label and then keep it at my house." Cheeky git, but I let him have it anyway.

Les was always loyal and when he took over from Terry Wogan on "Blankety Blank," he made sure that I was a guest on the show and that opened a few doors for me. In fact, not long after this, I appeared on BBC's "The Little and Large Show," and quite a few other guest spots followed.

One day, I got a phone call from Les asking for a favour. It was Meg's birthday and he was throwing a surprise party for her at a hotel in Lytham. He had booked one of his favourite singers, Billy Eckstine, to perform at the party and just wanted to enjoy himself with Meg: would I act as the host and perform the support spot for him? Of course I would. I jumped at the chance as it would be an honour to support such a big star, but mainly because it was Les who had asked.

I was now with a new manager, Roy Hastings, and over the next few years my TV work increased. I became a regular guest on "Des O'Connor Tonight." Des loved having comedians on the show, as we weren't there to plug a book or our latest film. He could ad-lib with us and have some fun. The show went out live and there was always a buzz around the studio. I had been booked and was watching the show the week before I was on. What a line up, they had: Freddie Starr, Oliver Reed and Stan Boardman. Freddie was, to say the least, difficult.

Oliver was drunk and referred to a part of his anatomy that he had just had a tattoo on. When Des asked where it was, Oliver replied, "On my Cock!" Des nearly died, but there was nothing he could do about it. Surely, Stan would behave himself? Well he didn't, he told a gag about Fokker airplanes. If you don't know what that gag was, I suggest you find it on You Tube. The show never went out live again and, so I had to record my appearance in advance with the ITV bosses in attendance checking every word I said. Nowadays, you hear a lot worse on TV, but back then it was shocking.

With my TV work taking off and my divorce finalised, I decided that it was time to buy myself a house. I mentioned this to Terry Alcock and he asked me that as he was looking to move would I be interested in his place? I had a look around it and, as it was in a nice area and in a very nice condition, I made him an offer that he was happy with and moved in. I now had my very own bachelor pad and it became a place where other acts would stop when they were in town working. As I was having lots of friends coming to the house, I built "Miller's Bar." It became well known in the business and was great for when I had barbecues.

A friend of mine, Peter Piper, was appearing at The Pleasure Beach, and was looking for somewhere to stop for the season. So, I offered to rent him a room and he moved in. After three days, I found a strange woman in my kitchen: he had moved his new girlfriend in without asking me, but I let that one go. Then, one night after I got home from working, there was a knock at the door. As I opened it, about ten girls pushed past me, saying they were here for the party. Shortly, Peter arrived, so I asked what was going on. He told me that he had arranged a Cheese and Wine party for the dancers. I wasn't happy that I hadn't even been asked. I told him that the party was off and to take his cheese out of the fridge and find somewhere else to eat it! But the final straw was when I came home to find the front door wide open and all the lights in the house on. When he came home, I confronted him about it. Apparently, he had had an argument with his girlfriend and stormed out leaving the door open. She had followed him. That was at 7.00pm and it was now 11.30pm. The time had come for him to move out and I got the house back to myself. I liked Peter and we are still friends, but I just couldn't live with him.

In 1987, I was signed up alongside Mike Smith and Cheryl Baker to co-present a Saturday evening show on ITV called "The Funny Side."

To promote the series, Granada TV took Cheryl Baker, Steve Leahy (the producer) and myself to "The Montreux TV Festival." It was very classy and very expensive, but we weren't paying for anything.

Steve Leahy took us to a very nice restaurant for dinner and Ted Robbins joined us. He is now a presenter on BBC Lancashire, but has been in so many TV series including "Phoenix Nights". He won't mind me saying that he is a larger-sized gentleman, so when he saw the size of the massive plates, his eyes lit up. Unfortunately, this was a Nouvelle Cuisine restaurant and the portions were very small. The main course arrived: it was a piece French toast with a small piece of squid delicately placed on top. Other diners were carefully nibbling away and commenting on how wonderful the food was, but not Ted. He just picked it up and put it all into his mouth and gulped it down in one go. I laughed, but I was the same, we weren't cut out for pretentious restaurants. After the meal, we were so hungry that we had to stop at a McDonalds on the way back to the hotel and I'm sure that we weren't the only ones.

The hotel was full of TV and music industry people, as the Montreux Music Festival was also being held at the same time. Now, I've met some famous people in my life and have to say that some of the nicest people I've met are the rock stars, but I'm still quite star-struck with these people. So when I found myself in a lift with Mick Hucknall from Simply Red, you can imagine how lost for words I was.

It happened when I was in the lift coming down from my room. It stopped to let someone else in. To my surprise it was Mick Hucknall and he instantly recognised me! He explained how he had fond memories of watching me on "The Comedians" with his dad. He was really nice to me and, as he was leaving the lift, he asked if I would join him at the bar for a drink. I was in awe of him and agreed to meet him there, but was a bit tongue-tied. So as the door was closing I found myself saying, "Cheers Simply!" I felt such a prat and couldn't face meeting him for that drink after making such a gaffe.

When I say the hotel was full of stars, I mean global stars. I was in the next bedroom to Whitney Houston! She had a security guard outside her door day and night. So, when I went to bed late, I felt sorry for this guy who had to sit there all night. I offered to make him a coffee, but he refused and told me to get to bed, I was only being friendly!

Back home, The Funny Side started its run, and was a typical Saturday night light entertainment show. We were getting 12-14 million viewers, but in those days, those figures just weren't good enough, so after one series, ITV decided not to re-commission it.

My lasting memory of that series was when we had the wrestler, Kendo Nagasaki on the show. I was dressed up as a wrestler and was to be thrown about a bit. If you remember, I had learned how to do wrestling falls back at Pontin's, but this was a bit different. The idea was for a member of the public to read wrestling moves from a book with Mike Smith. Kendo Nagasaki would then do the moves on me.

It was going well as I walked out in the costume and the audience laughed, but as soon as Kendo walked out, I knew I was in trouble. He was out to prove that wrestling was a serious sport. He wasn't being gentle with me at all as he slammed me on to the floor. I managed to fall correctly, but hadn't thought about my microphone pack, which was positioned in the small of my back. The pain I felt as it pushed into my back was agonising, but I had to carry on, as I didn't want to have to repeat the move in a retake. There is a bad quality clip of this on You Tube, which is worth a look at. At the end of the routine, Kendo picked up Mike Smith and spun him round, but he didn't slam him on to the floor! Maybe it was because Mike was wearing a very nice suit.

Chapter 10

Wendy and The War Years

In February of 1988, my life was about to change forever. I had been asked to perform in a charity show at The Queens Hotel in Blackpool. I arrived, ready to do the gig, but whilst I was waiting to go on, I got talking to Wendy. She was helping with the charity that night and I already knew her. She was now single and so was I, so the conversation went in a different direction than the earlier times we had met. I really liked her and it wasn't long before we started seeing each other on a regular basis. Soon after, she moved in with her youngest son, Julian. My bachelor pad was about to change beyond all recognition: she brought cushions! It wasn't long before we had new curtains and rugs. My house had become a home.

Wendy's eldest son, Michael, had been living down south, but moved to Blackpool before the summer. He was looking for a job and I was looking for someone to work with me. It was an obvious decision and he started in time for my summer season at Blackpool's South Pier. Tom O'Connor was topping the bill and he asked Michael to sell his merchandise whilst he was selling my tapes. This was ideal and we had a great season. However, unbeknown to us, Tom was being followed by reporters from the News of The World. They had a story about him and were trying to get some proof and some photos. It was a very bad time for Tom, as the papers were making all sorts of allegations about his private life and he had to defend his actions, because things weren't as they appeared on the surface.

The press hounded him and I started getting phone calls from journalists asking questions about him. Tom was a friend and I wasn't about to betray him to a Sunday newspaper. Michael was even drawn into the whole sordid affair, which was totally unfair as he was just a kid. Tom had to tell his wife that they were going to run the story the following Sunday and I felt so sorry for him as he couldn't even defend himself. I helped him as much as I could, but it very nearly destroyed him.

During that summer, Chubby Brown was also appearing at the South Pier Theatre in a late show. He really isn't anything like the character that he portrays on stage and some people can't understand that offstage, he is quiet and quite a private man. His dressing room was always open to members of our show and I would always call in for a chat. He became a regular visitor to my house on Sunday afternoons for barbecues. Luckily, we had nice weather that year, so Sundays were a great way to relax.

In January of 1989, I headed off to Australia for some shows. Wendy came with me and we loved every minute of it, but I didn't know how sneaky she could be. We returned home on 23rd February and slept for a day to get over the jet lag. It was then that Wendy told me that I had been booked for a corporate gig at The Queens Hotel in Blackpool on the 25th. It had been a last minute booking and although it was my birthday, I didn't want to let them down, so I got ready and headed off to the hotel.

The gig was in the small function room upstairs, but when I opened the door, it was in darkness. All of a sudden, the lights went on, and people popped up from their hiding places and started singing "Happy Birthday to you." I was taken aback by the surprise, but what got me most was that everyone was wearing bald wigs with long hair down the side, just like my hair! Wendy had managed to organise a surprise 40th Birthday party for me. I still don't know how she managed to do it, I mean, we'd been in Australia for nearly a month.

It was an amazing night, but it was difficult recognising people in those wigs. I was struggling to work out who some people were until they removed their wigs, but one person that I didn't have a problem with was Chubby Brown. He had written "F★★k Off" on the forehead of his wig! Apparently, he'd done that just minutes before I arrived and nearly ruined the surprise because everyone was laughing.

The Queens Hotel holds many good memories for me. Pat and Rudi Mancini owned it and were great hosts and great friends of mine. Their cocktail bar became the hang-out for many of the showbiz people who were in town. After Rudi's death a few years later, Pat spent a lot of her time raising money for local charities and was rightfully awarded both the CBE and an MBE for this work. Sadly, Pat passed away in 2011.

As we moved into the 1990's the world was full of conflict and our troops were involved in the 1st Gulf War. I was honoured to be asked to go to the region to entertain them and help keep morale up. I was asked to go to Saudi Arabia with Bradley Walsh, but before we went, we had to go through a training programme. There was a very real fear that chemical weapons could be used and we needed to be prepared. We learned how to use gas masks and other protective equipment that might be required.

We arrived in Saudi and were ferried to our hotel. We were dressed in our army camouflage kit, carrying our gas masks etc. when we were called to a room for a briefing. Saudi was in real danger, so we must carry our masks at all times and we must respect the country and their customs. As this was a Muslim country, amongst other things, we were told not to "look" at the women. It all seemed quite sensible and we were determined to behave ourselves.

When it was time for us to go to perform for the troops, we would be flown by helicopter to the location, which to me was much more frightening than the Iraqi threat! But when you are nervous, funny things happen. Bradley and I were in full kit complete with gas masks and things hanging from our belts. We were in the lift, on our way down to the ground floor, when it stopped at another floor to let some people in. These people turned out to be six, fully-veiled women. The doors to the lift closed and it continued its descent to the ground floor. All of a sudden, an alarm started ringing and I could feel the sense of panic setting in. As we reached the ground floor, the doors opened and we were greeted with a sight that I will never forget. There were men in Arabic robes pulled up to their waists, running towards the front door. I turned around to look at Bradley who was giggling like a schoolgirl in the corner of the lift. All he could say was, "They told us not to look at the women. I tried not to look at them!" He was stood looking into the corner of the lift, but his gas mask had inadvertently pressed the alarm button. It was only the lift alarm, but everyone had assumed it was a missile attack. I have never been so embarrassed in all my life.

After the successful shows in the Gulf, I was asked to go to other areas of the world where our troops were on active service. I've been lucky enough to go to places like Belize, The Falklands and Bosnia. All of these places have had their problems, but all of them are fantastic places in their own right.

I have been to The Falklands on several occasions and can confirm that it can be bloody cold! Which reminds me of the time I was there with Joe Pasquale. We were doing a show in a gym and they had set the stage up leaving a space behind it as a dressing room area. The seating area for the troops was set up as normal with benches for the rank and file soldiers and comfy armchairs at the front for the officers.

Now, like every other performer, I have to go to the toilet just before I go onstage, so I asked where it was. I was told to open the door, go outside and the toilets were in a block about 100 metres away. I was already in my stage suit and it was cold and raining heavily out there, so I had to think quickly. I had been drinking a beer from a pint glass, so this was the obvious answer. I went in the glass and then went on stage, but when I came off, there was no sign of the glass that I had left by the door. I looked all over for it, but it wasn't anywhere to be found.

Eventually, Joe came offstage so I asked him if he had seen the glass. To my utter horror, he said, "You mean that glass of water? I used it to fill up my bird hat." Now, I should explain that Joe used to start his act with a daft gag whilst wearing a hat with small birds on stalks that spun around. As they spun, they fired water out which would go all over the front row of the audience. You've guessed it: he had filled it up with my pee. I explained that to him and he looked at me straight in the face and said in his squeaky voice, "Oh my God, you've just pissed all over the top Johnnies!" I'm sure that they wouldn't have been amused, but I bet all the guys sat on the benches would have loved it.

I also worked with a comedy duo called "Dave and Amos" in The Falklands. These guys were so funny, but never made it big. I only had to look at them and I'd start laughing. We were all travelling inside an army vehicle that was linked together like a train. These things could go anywhere, but this one went somewhere we'd rather it hadn't. The driver made an error and the whole thing tipped over, injuring many of us on board. We were in quite a remote area and needed medical help quickly, which is when the British Army comes into its own. We were airlifted to the military hospital for treatment.

I had broken a couple of ribs and they hurt when I moved and especially if I laughed. So, with Dave and Amos in the room, I was in pain a lot. Amos was in the bed next to me and when Dave came to see him and told him about phoning home I couldn't hold my laughter back. They both had strong "West Country" accents, so whatever they said sounded funny at the best of times. "I've told my wife all about it and they are putting a banner up for when we return. It says, WELCOME HOME YOU BRAVE WOUNDED SOLDIERS." I could just picture the scene and kept laughing even though it hurt.

The journey back from the Falklands was usually broken by a stopover on the Ascension Islands. We were there when the giant turtles were laying their eggs and were offered the chance to go and witness this event. We were told to bring our cameras, but not to interfere in any way with the turtles as they were protected by law. I had seen things like this on wildlife programmes, but to see it in real life was too good a chance to miss. As it became dark, everyone from the show, including the band, was taken to the secluded beach and sure enough the turtles were there. We all took loads of photos and the army guys offered to get them processed for us in time for us leaving in the morning.

Musicians have a bit of a reputation when it comes to drinking and the bass player on this show more than lived up to it. He always seemed to be slightly drunk, but was never nasty and always played perfectly.

So, when we all received our photos in the morning, I was keen to see how he had done. Amazingly, he had twenty-four perfect photos from the night before, every single one of them was in perfect focus. The only problem was that every one of them was of a large tractor tyre! In his drunken state, turtles and tyres must have looked the same.

Whilst waiting for our flight back from Ascension with Joe Pasquale, we encountered a delay. As this was a military airport, there were no bars and nothing to do, so I pulled out a bottle of "Cane Juice." This is home-made illicit liquor that had been given to me on the trip. I poured Joe and myself a large one each in our teacups. We got chatting and with the aid of the cane juice, the time passed by quite quickly. Our flight was called and as we stood up, it hit us! We hadn't realised how strong it was and Joe was particularly giggly and wobbly. The military aren't used to seeing drunken people getting on to a plane, so when we were challenged about our sobriety, Joe piped up, "It wasn't me officer, it was that Mick Miller, he made me drink it!" The officer just laughed and let us board the plane. We were asleep in minutes and the long journey home didn't feel so bad.

I think that the saddest place I've been to entertain the troops has to be Bosnia. It is a beautiful country and most of the local people we met were so nice to us. The tragedy in this country was that it was the innocent civilians that were suffering. Ethnic cleansing knew no boundaries as men, women and children were being slaughtered. International forces were trying to protect them, but the horrors continued. Whilst we were there, we were given the chance to visit an orphanage where I was shocked at the conditions. I'm not going to go into what I saw there, but it brought me to tears.

On these trips, you get an officer to look after you and the one we had this time was fresh out of Sandhurst. He looked about twelve-years-old to me, but he was a fully-qualified officer. We had to drive along a road that was a known spot for snipers to attack and we knew that they were in the area. Before we set off, we had a briefing and were told that if we came under attack, the safest place to be was under the vehicles. Our armed guards would then be able to deal with the situation without worrying about us.

Despite the possibility of attack, I felt quite safe under the protection of the British Army. About half-way along the route, we stopped for a break and as we stood by the convoy having a cigarette, I heard a noise. It sounded like a bang, but I couldn't be sure as it was in the distance. So I turned around to ask our officer, but he was nowhere to be seen. The girls were there, the band were there, in fact everyone was there except Officer Sandhurst! I shouted out his name and he answered from under the Land Rover. Now, I thought he was there to look after us, but he was more interested in looking after himself. For the record, it wasn't a sniper attack, it was just a noise from a nearby farm.

The show was near a town called Gornji Vakuf and the morning after it I was stood outside having a fag when Officer Sandhurst walked up to me. I commented on how beautiful the lake was and he agreed. He then pointed to some ducks swimming on it and said, "Do you see those ducks" in his posh accent. He then went on to say, "Those are flightless ducks and you only get them in Bosnia." I couldn't resist it and said, "Well, where else are they going to go?" he didn't have an answer to that.

Perhaps one of the more bizarre incidents with the troops was in Belize. I was there to entertain our guys and girls, but didn't think about The Gurkhas in the audience. As I started my act, a translator stood up and started repeating everything I said in their language. I would get a laugh from the Brits, followed by a polite laugh from the Gukhas. It wasn't one of my best gigs, because I'm not good with Nepalese humour! But these guys are not to be messed with, as they are as hard as nails. It's a good job that they are on our side.

As I was about to leave Belize, I was presented with a ceremonial knife by the Gurkhas. It's called a Kukri and it is a great honour to be given one by them. I was humbled and I will never forget that day. They even gave me a book that explained everything you need to know about the knife and its traditions. But it wasn't until I got home and somebody asked me about it, that I realised I had been given a Kukri book!

These trips to war zones were always an adventure, but with Wendy now firmly ensconced in the house, I never knew what to expect on my return. She would use the time that I was away to decorate and improve the house. I got used to coming home to a new-look lounge or redecorated dining room. She loved home-making and was very good at it, but she excelled herself when I returned home and found that she had had workmen in and removed the staircase! There was a ladder leading up to the bedrooms, but that was only temporary, as the men were coming back to fit a new bespoke staircase in a few days. I've learned to trust her judgment, as she's never been wrong and the house was always nicer than it had been before.

Chapter 11

Fun In The Sun – Home and Abroad

After doing many more shows for the troops, I was working back in the UK. Wendy had surpassed her previous best as I returned home and went to hang my coat up in the under-stairs cupboard as normal only to find that it was now a toilet! The house had been almost completely remodelled by now, so it was only a matter of time before we would need to move so that she could work her magic on somewhere else. In the meantime, life and work went on.

I had known The Nolan Sisters for a long time, and had worked with Linda Nolan many times. She had become known as "The Naughty Nolan" and we both were regular guests on James Whale's late night TV show. So when she became the star of "Maggie May's" on Central Pier, she asked me to be her special guest. I enjoyed three great summer seasons there with her and we had some great support acts over those three years.

After that, the opportunity came up to host my own comedy night in the "Merrie England Bar" at the North Pier. I was a bit apprehensive as the venue had a bad reputation. It was a magnet for drunken yobs and I certainly didn't want to be part of that scene. I went to a meeting with First Leisure, who owned the venue, to discuss the possibilities and they told me that they wanted to rebrand it as "Mick Miller's Comedy Store". They would have a strict door policy and everything would be fine.

I thought about it and, on the condition that the drunken idiots wouldn't be allowed in, I agreed to do it. After a few teething problems the venue opened and I arrived for the opening night. I was pleased when I was told that the venue was almost full and I ventured in. That pleasure turned to pain as I looked at the audience: there were about twenty blokes in one corner all dressed as Vikings. The opposite corner was full of male nuns and about three Andy Pandys were dotted about the room. As I stood there, they started football chants and hurled abuse at each other. There was no way anyone could perform comedy to this audience, so I turned around and walked back outside and asked the doorman to fetch the venue manager. He looked so pleased with himself as he proudly told me how full it was, but he wasn't so proud when I told him I was going home. I explained that I had only agreed to do this venue if the drunks weren't allowed in. I told him that he would have to get them out and make sure that anyone who had a stupid massive hat would have to remove it so people behind them could see. After all, this was meant to be a proper comedy night out, not a slanging match with very drunk people. He laughed at first because he thought I was joking, but when I got in my car and drove off, he stopped laughing.

About three quarters of an hour later my phone rang. It was one of the high-up First Leisure bosses asking me to come back down to the venue as it was all sorted out. So I set off back and, as I arrived, the manager, who seemed a little flustered, greeted me. "Have you got it sorted?" I asked. He assured me that it was fine now and led me into the room. It wasn't as full, but it was a lot quieter and there were no football chants. I thanked him and went on to do the show. It wasn't a great night, but it was okay.

The whole season there was a bit of a nightmare as the room was very difficult to work. The stage was in a bad position and sections of the audience couldn't even see it. I wasn't ever happy there and, as the season ended, I was quite relieved. It just wasn't my sort of venue. However, Joey Blower has been very successful there and with hard work has made it his own.

The following year, Central Pier decided to go with a comedy format. The show was promoted by Roger Davis and featured Chrissie Rock, Johnnie Casson, Albi Senior and myself. I was back in my comfort zone and enjoying what I was doing. On one of my days off, I decided to go up to Troon to see "The Open Golf Championship". A friend of mine who was a famous Lancashire comedian decided to come with me. "Wandering Walter" is a legend in Lancashire, but never normally left the county. In fact, when he was asked to do a gig at Knutsford in Cheshire, his reply was, "I don't go that far on my holidays, why should I go that far to work?" So a trip to Troon was a big adventure for him. We only went for the day and he sent fifty postcards!

We were still living in the same house and although we were still happy there, we were actively looking for a new place. The Sunday afternoon barbecues were still going on much to my neighbours' annoyance. Brian Conley, Bradley Walsh and Chubby Brown were regular guests and maybe it did get a bit noisy at times, but never on purpose.

The only downside to the house was the garden. We were quite near the sea and nothing grew very well. Wendy really wanted a nice garden. It took a while, but we found the perfect house in Poulton-le-Fylde, which is just outside Blackpool. We are still there and still very happy in that house.

The winter months can be long and when an opportunity to work abroad on a regular basis came up, I jumped at the chance. A guy from Tenerife called David Elliot had got in touch with Roy Hastings and asked if I would be prepared to work at a large cabaret venue out there. Roy knew the place, as he had a home on the island. David was the Resort Manager for Thompson Holidays and they wanted to offer a night out with a full show for their guests.

"Exit Palace" was a 700-seat cabaret venue and already had a full show in place. I would top the bill for one night when Thompson would take over the place. It sounded good and the money was very good too. Then Airtours got in touch as they wanted to do the same deal for their guests, so it became too good to turn down. I would fly down on a Monday, work two days during the week and fly home on Fridays to do weekend work in the UK.

The show was amazing and featured a full team of Spanish dancers, Mexican acrobats and a French magician. I arrived for the first show and was shown to my dressing room. It was basic, but comfortable, and had its own toilet which was good as I had "Spanish tummy." I immediately dived in there and sat down. There was an open window quite high up which had metal bars across it. As I sat there contemplating, I nearly jumped up and hit the ceiling as a tiger appeared at the window and let out a loud roar. It turned out to be part of the magic act, and it lived in a cage that backed up to my toilet window. I wasn't very happy about this, as I am an animal lover and believe that tigers should be left in the wild and not in a cage. I do have to say that it was very well looked after but, nevertheless, I would rather that it hadn't been there.

Tenerife was very good to me and I enjoyed several winters working out there. I had the best of both worlds: nice weather during the week and good paying gigs in the cold UK at the weekends. The duty-free fags and booze were a bonus. But I'm not a good flyer and as I had to fly to and from Tenerife every week I needed someone to travel with me. Bill Davenport was working with me at the time, so he accompanied me on the trips. He was a bit of a sun-worshiper, so he was in his element.

All good things come to an end and the holiday companies changed the way they ran their resorts. New managers were recruited and the cabaret nights didn't fit in with the new ways of thinking. So, sadly, they didn't renew my contract for another winter season. We had been playing to near capacity audiences and getting great reviews, but I totally understood that they wanted new things for their guests and was happy to move on to new things. It would have been easy to just carry on working over there, but I would have had to work in less prestigious venues and they wouldn't have been able to pay the money that I had been getting. So it was time to get back to the cold winters.

I still enjoy holidays in Tenerife and always meet up with my friends when I'm over there. David Elliot now has a bar/nightclub called Leonardo's and one time when I was over there he was holding a charity night. I agreed to do a short comedy spot for him and, when I arrived, I was told a friend was sat outside waiting to see me. When I went out Ken Dodd was sat at a table with his girlfriend. I've known them for years, but I wasn't expecting to see them there. He's a lovely man and I really look up to him as possibly the greatest comedian ever. I've said it before and I will say it again. Go and see him live in a theatre near you, but be prepared for a long show.

Chapter 12

The Flying Wok

I enjoy what I do and getting laughs is possibly one of the best feelings in the world, but I do also enjoy a bit of cooking. Unusually, the two things came together over two summers whilst working on the Haven Holiday circuit.

I had been booked to do the "Haven Holiday" centres along with their sister sites, "British Holidays." Several acts were booked as the Star Cabaret and we would move around the sites on a weekly rotation. Accommodation would be provided on site and the whole tour would take us around the country three times.

As the start of the season drew closer, I realised that due to the mileage involved, I was going to need someone to work with me and share the driving. I knew that Chubby Brown was ill with throat cancer and wasn't working. So I contacted Steve Cowper, who had worked with Chubby for sixteen years. I asked him if he was doing anything whilst Chubby was recuperating. He wasn't and was just on a small retainer wage. So I asked him if he would like to work with me for the summer months. He agreed and started the following week.

The first gig was up in Berwick-upon-Tweed and we arrived in the afternoon and were given the keys to a caravan. It was very nice and we settled in. I had brought some bacon and bread for breakfasts and lots of other food in a cool box to last us for the week. That evening after eating we headed over to the main entertainment complex where I would be working.

The room was full of a mixture of adults and children, which can be difficult. Peter Kay does a routine about kids on the dance floor at weddings: well that is just what you expect with kids at comedy shows in holiday parks! They slide across the dance floors and fire pretend Tommy Guns at you. To be honest, it was a bit daunting and I wondered if I had made the wrong decision in taking this work. As it happened, the kids were well-behaved and I didn't have any problems.

After the show the Entertainments Manager bought Steve and I drinks and we sat back-stage chatting to the entertainment team. They were all quite young and were keen to get into the entertainment business. They lived on the site in shared caravans and worked long hours. As we chatted, I found out that they were on a low wage and had to pay for electric and gas in their caravans. They weren't complaining, but I did feel a bit sorry for them. As we carried on, I realised that they weren't eating properly and just grabbed a burger when they could. I think I came over all paternal, as I remembered all the food that I had brought with us. We also had a case of beer in the boot of the car, so I decided to invite them all back to our caravan for some food and drinks. I just cooked everything we had and served it up. The team was so grateful and couldn't thank us enough, but it wasn't a problem as Steve and I had really enjoyed their company.

The following day, we set off to the next site via the supermarket where we stocked up on food and drinks. Throughout the week, we continued entertaining holidaymakers and feeding the entertainment teams. Soon, word got round, and we found ourselves the centre of attention as soon as we arrived on site. So, I decided that the best way forward was to shop each day and buy plenty of rice, vegetables and chicken. I also bought a big wok to cook it all in.

As we travelled around the country, Steve would print out an invitation for the team to join us in our caravan for supper and to bring some booze. It was good fun and, as a former Blue Coat, I knew what it was like for these youngsters. I felt I was giving something back to those who were just starting out. I think they appreciated what we did. Not every site got the "Flying Wok" treatment, because on Thursdays we would travel straight home after the show, so sorry to those who missed out.

During that season we met some great people: some have managed to make a career out of being entertainers, others have moved into management and caravan sales and some even turned up on TV talent shows. We still bump into some of these people and they always refer to The Flying Wok.

With the summer run coming to an end, Steve had a meeting with Chubby's management. They had a big disagreement and he parted company with them and Chubby. We had been getting on well together and he had been very good at making sure everything ran smoothly for me. I soon asked him to work for me full-time.

We did a second summer for Haven Holidays, but this time they decided to build a show around the guest stars. Each site would perform the same show and that would include the guest in the middle of the show. It was a great idea and worked very well. The Flying Wok was back and the teams were queuing up to be fed.

As you can imagine, not everything ran smoothly and mostly it was to do with our accommodation. I should explain that most sites have one or two old caravans put aside for the travelling cabaret acts. Unfortunately, some of these acts didn't respect their accommodation and left them in a right state. As part of my contract, Steve and I were supposed to get "Guest" accommodation and not a "Cabaret Van." Don't get me wrong, we did understand that at the height of the season, there might sometimes be a problem over this due to over-booking and we were prepared to muck in and accept the cabaret van. What we certainly wouldn't put up with was dirty cabaret vans. I just couldn't understand how much mess some people could make in just one night. Some of them were so bad that Steve wouldn't even let me look inside them. He would go straight back with the key and refuse to stop there.

I will never forget the time that we turned at one of the sites, which I won't name, and Steve went to find the Entertainments Manager who had the key to our accommodation. This particular manager had a bit of a reputation: she was not one to be messed with. So when she handed the key to Steve with a look of disdain on her face, Steve was not impressed. He said, "This isn't a cabaret van is it?" and she said, "It's what you have been given." So we headed off to what turned out to be a chalet-type unit. It was filthy, the beds had been slept in, the sheets were stained, the bins were full of takeaway curry cartons and the ashtrays were overflowing. We just turned around and left the room. Steve went in search of the Entertainments Manager and when he found her, she was dressed as a bear! This was a character for the children's show, as she was about to take that role in that afternoon's show. Steve was very polite to her and pointed out that the accommodation was filthy and that we shouldn't be stopping in a "Cabaret unit." She then went off on one, telling Steve that it wasn't a Cabaret Unit and that we should accept what we were given as we were "just cabaret!" Steve pointed out that if it were for her, she wouldn't stop in that unit, as it was filthy. She basically told Steve that we were being fussy and to put up with it. Now, I'm not a coward, but I was hiding around the corner. Steve changed his normal friendly demeanour and argued with her. Other members of staff, along with some of her entertainments team, were also hiding around corners and everyone was stifling their laughter. She wasn't very popular and nobody dare stand up to her. But the thing that made everyone laugh was when Steve said, "I'm sorry, but I'm not standing here wasting my time arguing with a bear." He went on to say, "We're not stopping here to be talked to like this, we're leaving." She didn't know what to say as he turned away. She demanded that we stop and do what she said because she was in charge or else she would call head office to report us. Steve just looked back at her and said, "When you call them, ask for Pete Allen (who booked us and was a good friend of mine) and tell him that we had turned up to work, you were very rude to us, so we left" and with that, we got into the car and drove out of the site. We knew that we would get a phone call from Pete and, sure enough, before we'd got out of the long drive, he rang. He saw the funny side and explained that as the site was full, this was the only accommodation available, but it should have been cleaned. He asked us to give it half an hour and then return when it would have been cleaned.

Half an hour later, we returned to find the entertainments manager cleaning the chalet. She was not happy, but still insisted that this wasn't a cabaret unit, so Steve opened a cupboard to reveal a sign saying, "TO ALL CABARET ACTS. PLEASE LEAVE THIS UNIT AS YOU FIND IT." She didn't have an answer to that one!

Another site in the South East had a bit of a reputation, so we were already wary when we arrived. As usual Steve picked up the key and a map showing us where the caravan was. From the outside it looked okay, but Steve said appearances can be deceptive and he would check it out before I went in. I sat in the car whilst he ventured in. I looked up just as he came back out of the door with a pained look on his face. He locked the door and got back into the car. It turned out that the caravan vas nice, but there was a drain problem. The whole place smelled of sewage. So we headed back and explained the situation and, to be fair, they apologised as they weren't aware of the problem. Unfortunately, there was only a cabaret van left. We had no choice other than to accept it. Steve gingerly opened the door and went in. It turned out to be a very old caravan with cream bench seating, but at least it was clean.

At this point, I should tell you that I liked to sleep on the bench seats in the lounge, as I like to watch the TV until quite late. There were some cushions on the seats, so I moved them to get comfortable. I got the shock of my life when I saw that they were covering up a huge bloodstain! So, I covered it up with a sheet and tried to forget it. As I relaxed, it was getting closer to the time for work and Steve was getting ready. Suddenly, I heard him laughing loudly, so I shouted through to ask what was so funny, but he just said that I would find out. I was puzzled, but soon found out when I had a shower. I pulled the curtain across and started laughing. I now saw what Steve had seen. The shower curtain looked like the one from the film, "Psycho". It was ripped to shreds as if someone had slashed it with a knife. It did make me wonder what had gone on in that caravan.

But the funniest story ever to do with caravans happened at a site near Clacton. Working at this site involved a long drive to get there and we were always tired. So after the show I just headed back to the caravan to catch up on some sleep. The Flying Wok never came out here, as we were always just too tired to do it. The site was very nice and we were always given good caravans to stop in. In this particular instance, the van was spectacular. It had a proper three-piece suite, an electric Aga-type cooker, wooden beams on the ceiling and an en suite bathroom in the master bedroom. It even had a proper washing machine in the kitchen. It was simply the best caravan we had ever been in: we couldn't believe our luck.

There was a late film on the TV, so I settled down to watch it and Steve went to bed. Eventually, I dozed off and slept like a log, but was rudely awoken about 7.30am. The caravan appeared to be rocking! But as it was early and I had just woken up, I couldn't work out what was happening. Things were going around in my mind as I tried to make sense of the situation. My first thought was that Steve must have gone back out and brought a girl back to the caravan. I thought that the rocking might be them "enjoying themselves." But then I heard voices outside, as the caravan seemed to bounce up and down. I was now more awake, so I opened the door. I don't know who got the biggest shock as

I stood there in just my boxer shorts. There were several blokes with a tractor and they had hooked it up to the caravan and had started to pull it away.

Well, you can imagine the look on their faces when they saw me. It turned out that this caravan was being repossessed, as the people that had bought it hadn't made any payments. These blokes weren't aware that we had been allocated it for one night and had already disconnected the gas, electric and drainage from the outside, as it was being moved to a secure pound. My thoughts turned to Steve who was unaware of what was going on, so I shouted through to him to come through to the front to see what was going on. Unfortunately, he was sat on the toilet, so he was told not to flush until they connected the sewage pipe back up! He had thought that the rocking was due to wind.

We were given half an hour to pack up and leave because they needed to get it moved before 9.00am, as the tractor was needed elsewhere after that. We weren't very happy, but did as we were told and left. As we drove off, we started laughing: it was the thought of us sat in a caravan as it was being towed away. We had a vision of Steve sat on the toilet reading the newspaper and me cooking breakfast as we trundled past everyone on the site. It's a good job we have a sense of humour.

There were times when the kids in the audience could be challenging to say the least! So, one of the entertainments managers had her own way of keeping them in control. Coral was in charge at a site in Great Yarmouth and what a character she was. She was a bit older than most of the team members on the circuit and had been in the business for a long time. She had been a dancer and was very proud of her legs: in fact she would tell everyone that she had "The best legs in showbiz." Don't get me wrong, she wasn't being serious, she just loved the banter.

Well, as I mentioned earlier, given half a chance, the kids would be running and sliding across the dance floor in front of the stage. As you can imagine, this was quite distracting for both the audience and me. So most sites put members of the team at the side of the dance floor to try and stop this happening. But Coral had grander ideas. She knew how annoying this could be, so she dealt with it in her own way. I don't know where it all came from, but she had barriers and cones that went around the dance floor: it looked like a set of road works, but it did the job.

One night, I was in mid flow when a young girl shouted out, "I know a joke." So, like a fool, I brought her on stage. She was probably around ten-years-old with long blonde hair and looked like a little angel. I thought it would be okay to let her tell her joke and, after chatting to her, I gave her the microphone. She was very confident, and started by saying, "A black cockerel was walking down the road, how many eyes did it have?" I hadn't a clue where this was going as I answered, "Two." She then said, "A white pussy cat came round the corner and followed it down the road. What was its name?" I still didn't see where this was going as I replied, "I don't know." To my utter horror, she then said, "Why do you know more about black cocks than white pussies!" The room went silent: I went very red and didn't know what to say. Then, I heard Steve laughing out loud from backstage. It seemed like ages, but must have only been a few seconds before the audience started laughing. Here am I being upstaged by a ten-year-old kid telling a blue gag, when, as part of my contract, I had to be squeaky clean.

As the laughter subsided, I tried to carry on, but by now had got the giggles: I just couldn't follow that joke. I ushered the kid offstage, but by now I had gone. There was no way I could carry on as I just kept laughing. The more I laughed, the more the audience laughed, so I figured that the best thing to do was go straight into the Noddy routine and get off. I even struggled to get that routine out which had never been a problem. So, I learned a valuable lesson that night, never trust cute kids!

Chapter 13

A New Direction

The holiday parks filled up the work diary and I could have carried on doing them as long as I wanted, but I was getting restless. Times were changing and young comedians were all that TV seemed to want, but I knew that I still had a lot to give and I was still ambitious. Out of the blue, a couple of interesting projects came up, but they didn't impress Roy Hastings. One was a pilot for a Radio 4 comedy series about an Ice Cream seller. The other was a TV Show for Ch 4 and E4, but neither of them were paying much money, so Roy Hastings (my manager) didn't want me to do them, but I was looking at the bigger picture.

A talented Manchester-based writer called Carl Cooper wrote the radio series and he had gathered a cast of great comedians in all the main roles. Amongst them was Toby Hadoke who ran a Comedy Club called "XS Malarkey" in Manchester. After the recording we got chatting about the club and I was impressed to find out that he ran it as a non-profit venture and gave new talent a chance to work with more established comedians. I offered to do the gig for him for a nominal fee, just to see if I was able to work to a young comedy club crowd.

On the night, I was on with two other comedians who would become good friends. Peter Slater is a character comedian and now runs his own comedy night at "The Lass O'Gowrie" pub in Manchester. Alfie Joey now presents the breakfast show on BBC Radio Newcastle. The show was amazing: Toby had been very supportive to me as I had been quite nervous about doing this gig. He reassured me that I would "go down a storm" and to do as long or as short a set as I wanted. I thought I might only do about twenty minutes, but Toby was right and I did well over an hour.

After the gig I was on a high and now knew that I was still relevant as a comedian. I realised that I was worth more than the gigs that I was getting. I still had ambition, but I was just treading water. I was working, but I was going nowhere.

The TV show was called, "Kings of Comedy" and was similar to "Big Brother." It was to feature a mix of eight comedians from both sides of the so-called divide. We all had to live together in a Big Brother-style house and perform routines. A public vote would decide who was evicted each week.

Stan Boardman, David Copperfield and myself were the "Mainstream" comedians and Andrew Maxwell, Ava Vidal, Janey Godley, Scott Capurro and Boothby Graffoe represented the new breed. The show was presented by Russell Brand and produced by Big Brother producers, Endemol.

As the weeks went on, we had to perform to an invited audience. Each week had a different theme, but it became obvious to me that the audiences were always the same young people. I was doing well, but I thought that it was unfair to us older guys always having to work to the new breed's regular type of audience. I made my feelings known and the next week we walked out to a bunch of pensioners. It was very funny to see the shocked faces on the younger comedians.

Then, they surprised us all when we had to perform to children, but it was Andrew Maxwell who impressed me during that week. He was normally a very political comedian, but turned into a perfect children's entertainer. He was a revelation.

The final week came all too soon and I came third. I was over the moon with that. Stan Boardman was second and the worthy winner was Andrew Maxwell. I still keep in touch with him and Janey Godley from the new breed comedians and, of course Stan and David were already friends.

In the months that followed, I began feeling that I wasn't happy with the work that I was being given by Roy Hastings. Things weren't right between us and I knew in my own mind that the time was coming for us to part company. I had proved that I could work to a younger audience and that I could hold my own with the new breed of young comedians, but I was still being marketed as the guy from "The Comedians." I was paying a 25% commission for management and I didn't really feel that I was being managed.

Jethro, the Cornish comedian, once said to me that he left his manager when he realised that at 25% commission, every fourth year, he was just working for his manager! All of these things were going around in my head and I had a decision to make. I spoke to Steve and asked his opinion. I also asked if he would be able to look after me, as there are so many things that need taking care of that you don't even think about. For example, I was VAT registered and I needed to know that things like that could be dealt with.

I spoke to Wendy and came to the decision that I had to leave Roy and go my own way. He had made me a director of his company, but I had never had any benefits from that position, so the first thing that I did was resign from that post. Then I wrote to Roy to explain that I was leaving his management. It was hard, but I knew that it was something that I had to do.

Straight away Steve had a website built, and we set about the task of letting everyone know that I was no longer with Roy Hastings. Almost immediately the phone started ringing with offers of work. The e-mails started flowing and I was up and running. Steve set about building up an Internet presence and we even had a MySpace page. The difference became glaringly obvious: I was now in the 21st century.

We had hit the ground running and I was happy with the new direction I was taking. Steve was looking after all the business side of things as well as working with me on the gigs. Things were going well and I had made some new friends within the new comedy scene. Andrew Maxwell asked me to be a guest on his regular comedy night at the famous "Comedy Store" in London. It was a midnight show and I was a bit apprehensive, but Steve thought it would be a good experience and encouraged me to accept the gig. Deep down, I knew that I could do it as I had done so well at XS Malarkey, so I agreed.

Don Ward, who has been very influential to many comedians, owns the Comedy Store. He knows the comedy business inside out and his club is a great place to work. Lots of comedians end up there after working in and around the capital and are stood at the bar watching the shows. I went down really well and then went out front to watch the rest of the show. Don congratulated me on my set and told us to watch the new comedian who was on next. It was a very strange young guy wearing a ladies' leather coat and make up. Don was predicting big things for him, so I thought I should see what he did. Steve and I watched in amazement as this guy went through his very surreal act. I really wasn't sure about him, but he seemed like a nice guy.

About two months later, I was sat at home watching TV when I thought that I recognised the comedian on a new show. I phoned Steve and asked if he was watching the programme. He wasn't, but turned over and checked. I was right, it was the guy from that night at The Comedy Store. It was Noel Fielding in "The Mighty Boosh." Noel has gone on to be one of the biggest names in comedy and when we bumped into him at The Groucho Club in London about a year later he remembered me and we ended up chatting for ages. I have to say that he had matured and his fame certainly hadn't gone to his head.

Since then I have also worked at the Manchester Comedy Store, which is fantastic. Don has pumped a lot of money into these clubs and I urge you to give them a try if you can. There are some very good comedians on the comedy club circuit and you just might see one of tomorrow's big stars before they are famous.

Putting myself in these venues and meeting these people could only be good for me. It made me work more on my material and sharpened up my act. You never know who is watching and that can also be good for you. Out of the blue I got a phone call from Justin Moorhouse who had been in "Phoenix Nights" with Peter Kay. Justin was the one who had his face painted as a tiger. He is now a presenter on Manchester's Key 103 radio and he loved what I did. He wondered if I would come along to perform at his charity show at The Opera House in Manchester. It was to raise funds to help premature babies, as his child had been premature and he wanted to give something back to the Special Baby Care Unit that helped them so much. I thought it was a good cause and that he was very genuine in what he was doing, so I immediately agreed.

It wasn't until I arrived at the theatre that I found out who else was on the bill. In fact the show had sold out without them announcing any of the acts, so the audience hadn't a clue who was on. They had a treat in store, because Justin had pulled a great line-up together: Coronation Street stars, Anthony Cotton and Sally Lindsay; young Manchester-based comedians like Alfie Joey; Jimmy Carr even travelled up from

London and then went straight back after the show; John Thompson from "The Fast Show" and stars from Phoenix Nights including Paddy McGuinness and Peter Kay. I was the only one there I hadn't heard of! Peter was very complimentary about me and even said that he was nervous about going on after me.

I had a chat with Peter who told me that I was one of his favourite comedians and that he had been to see me in Tenerife, but was too shy to come up to say hello. We got on really well and I asked him to bear me in mind if he was ever going to do another sitcom. To my surprise, he told me that there had been a part for me in "Max & Paddy," but he had phoned Roy Hastings who had told him I wasn't interested. So I think I did the right thing in leaving him.

The show got rave reviews and they were praising me: apparently I was the highlight of the night. I couldn't believe it, but I have to admit that I felt really proud as to how well I had done. I was sure that this night would do me nothing but good and I was right because, not long after, I got a phone call asking me if I would be interested in reading for a part in "IDEAL." This was a show that I had been watching on BBC3 and starred Johnny Vegas as a small-time drug dealer in Salford. It sounds like a strange idea for a comedy programme, but it really worked.

The show was co-produced by Steve Coogan's Baby Cow production company and the BBC. I soon found myself at the BBC's Oxford Rd. studios in Manchester with a script to read from. I was nervous because I am dyslexic and find reading straight from a script very difficult, but they seemed to like me. I was asked back to do a read through with Johnny and immediately offered the part of Keith who was Johnny's character's stepfather. I was amazed, but Johnny told me that he had really wanted me for the role.

The deal was done and Steve asked for scripts well in advance so I had time to learn them, as I didn't want to let anyone down. Johnny was great with me, he helped me settle back into acting, something I hadn't done since "Scully's New" Year" all those years ago. The writer, Graham Duff, was lovely and seemed to write in a style that I found easy to work with, but he had a mischievous streak, because every now and then he would put in lines that were tongue-twisters. Both Johnny and I would struggle with lines like, "I'm off to buy fifty, faulty, four-slot toasters." That took a few takes!

We filmed it at the BBC in Manchester and I loved every minute of it. The whole cast and crew was like a family and Johnny was at the centre of it. He is a smoker and the law says that the dressing rooms are in a working environment and therefore NO SMOKING. So Johnny had an idea. He brought a camper van into the car park outside the studio. This wasn't inside the BBC and was his own personal space so he could smoke. In fact, most of us smokers would be in there at one time or another.

Unfortunately, after seven series, BBC3 got a new controller called Zai Bennet, who decided to cancel the show. Unbelievably, "IDEAL" had been getting its highest viewing figures ever. The show was loved by many and various groups were set up to try and get the decision reversed, but it was not to be. I have to admit that I was really upset by the news. It had been a great part of my life and I was going to miss it. It was shown all over the world and when I was on a cruise ship in the Pacific, an Australian guy came up to me and asked if I was Keith from IDEAL. When I told him that I was, he called all his mates over and said, "It IS him!" I couldn't buy a drink for days. They insisted on buying them for me. It's amazing to see where IDEAL is shown and when I get my royalty payments from Australia, America and even Israel, I have to pinch myself.

The economic downturn hit everybody and entertainment is always the first thing that people cut back on. I had been doing a lot of corporate work, especially company golf days. But when money becomes tight cutbacks have to be made and these events are the first things to be stopped. I went from doing three a week during the summer months to maybe three over the whole summer, so we had to look at other potential work opportunities.

Cruise ships were still doing well, as the prices had come down and were now affordable for the working man. I made the decision to do more cruise work and it has been very good to me. I have travelled the world and had some great times. But as you can imagine, I have a host of stories about the people you meet.

One morning, I sat in a lounge area next to an elderly lady. We started chatting and she told me how much she had enjoyed my show. She was a lovely lady and I was surprised to find out that she was ninety and travelling alone. Out of the blue, she asked if I had any influence on board the ship, as she needed something. I explained that I didn't have any special privileges, but I would try to help if I could and asked what she wanted. She said, "Could you see if you can get me the results from Catford Dog Racing Track as I had a few bets before we left England." I had to smile, because if I make it to ninety, I hope I'll be just like her. I did manage to get the results, but never did find out if she had won.

I also bumped into this lady on another day. I sat down with her and as we chatted another lady joined us. This woman looked quite ill and was obviously suffering from seasickness. Quick as a flash, my new friend asked if that was what was wrong. The other woman confirmed this as she continued to look very ill. So, my friend called the waiter over and asked for a spoonful of raspberry jam. The other woman looked puzzled as my lady explained by saying, "You should take a spoonful of raspberry jam when you feel seasick as it does help." The jam arrived and the woman ate it and asked if it would stop her from feeling sick. "No dear, but it will make it taste better when you throw up" was her reply. I could hardly contain my laughter and couldn't work out whether she was being serious or just joking.

Some people say things that are just plain stupid. I was talking to a couple when an announcement was made over the ship's tannoy system. It was the Captain and he was informing everyone that we were just about to cross over the equator. This couple was so excited by this news and just had to get outside as quickly as possible so that they could take a photograph of it. Now, is it just me, but doesn't one piece of sea look much the same as the next. I think that they were expecting a big sign, or a line on the sea! I also regularly get asked if I stop on the ship after my show. Well, when you are in the middle of the Pacific, it would be one hell of a swim back to shore!

Despite all of the silly stuff, I really enjoy my cruise work. It really annoys me when Simon Cowell refers to some acts as being, "Like something you would find on a cruise ship," because entertaining cruise passengers is not an easy job. There are strict rules on what you can and can't say or do as a "guest entertainer" and those rules are even stricter for the resident entertainers. The cruise companies are very protective of their brands.

My only problem with the cruise work is the flying. I'm not a good flyer and I'm sure I'm not alone, but it's just something that I have to do. People think that I live a glamorous life, travelling to exotic destinations throughout the world, but the truth is that I rarely get to see any of the sights. I generally arrive at an airport and am met by a local Port Agent who takes me straight to the ship. But occasionally, I do get off at a port if there is something I want to see. Many years ago, I was working on one particular ship that was docking in Acapulco. I had not gone down well with some of the more snooty people on board and was feeling bad about it.

I had decided to get off the ship and go to see the famous cliff divers. They are amazing and, as I queued, I could hear some of the passengers saying things about me. They were saying they didn't know who I was and that they should have more famous entertainers on board instead of me. But as we reached the divers, things were about to change, because one of the Mexican divers took one look at me and shouted, "Hey, its Mick Miller!" and called me over to him. He was also calling the other divers over to meet me, "This is the famous Mick Miller," he said. Well that shut the snobs up as I heard one of them say, "He must be very famous if they know him in Mexico." I didn't have the heart to tell them that I knew this guy from the previous summer season, when he was with the stunt diving team that performed at Blackpool Pleasure Beach and that we used to have a drink together in a local late-bar. These snobby people now thought that I was an internationally-known entertainer, who was probably a big star in Central America. Isn't it funny how people can change their opinion of you in seconds?

Steve does all the deals and contracts for the cruise work, but he doesn't come on the ships with me. So when the opportunity to work on one of the farewell voyages of the QE2 came along, he decided to check out the possibility of him being allowed to travel with me. Our Cruise Agent, Jo Martin, checked with Cunard and it was fine with them. By this time, the QE2 was looking a bit tired as it was at the end of its service, but it was still an impressive ship. To be able to have been on her is something that you will remember for life.

Where would the cruise go? How long would we be on board? How hot would it be? These questions were on our mind, but when we found out that we would be joining in Newcastle and getting off the next day in Edinburgh, it was a little disappointing. At least Steve managed to sail on the most famous cruise liner in the world.

Chapter 14

By Royal Appointment and Beyond

Things were going well and even though the economic climate was tough, I was still working hard. My TV work had helped my profile and I was doing a lot of corporate work. The after dinner work was coming in and cabaret work was still quite good. Summer Seasons were a thing of the past, but regular one-night shows were still possible in some resorts. Blackpool was one of these resorts and, as I was now living in Poulton-le-Fylde, I was ideally placed to be part of this. My mate, Tony Jo, was convinced that old-style variety shows still had an audience and put his money where his mouth was when The North Pier theatre became available.

Blackpool has two distinct types of visitors: older people and families during the week and younger stag and hen parties at the weekends. So, Tony decided to offer a package of shows to fit the bill. The owners of the pier were impressed with what he had to offer and he signed a deal with them. One of his shows was to be a Comedians-style show and he wanted me to be part of it. The comedy legend, Frank Carson, topped the bill. The show did very well and I really enjoyed working with Frank again.

At this point I have to tell you about Frank Carson. He lived about two miles from me and was such a lovely man. He was never offstage, as he would always be telling jokes to anyone that he met. He would often phone me up and do fifteen minutes of gags before I could get a word in. When he finally took a breath I would ask him if he had phoned for a reason. Sometimes he had, but other times he had dialled the wrong number and thought he was talking to his mate, Victor. Sometimes he just forgot what he was calling for, so he did some more gags. I loved Frank and when he died recently I felt a great loss. He was in his mid-eighties and had the energy of someone half his age. Frank was probably the last of the great gag tellers: there will never be another one like him.

The North Pier shows were a big success and Tony decided to do it again the next year. I was part of a Comedians show again and was very happy to be involved. Business was good and Blackpool seemed to be changing for the better.

Of course, I was still working all year round. I was filming Ideal, working on the cruise ships along with after dinner and cabaret work. It was now 2010 and Paul Boardman (son of Stan) had the idea of taking some of us on the road again. The shows were doing okay, but the bigger picture was to film a 40th Anniversary DVD in 2011. So, Paul booked Blackpool Grand Theatre for a short run of shows on Fridays during August of that year. Stan Boardman, Frank Carson, Jim Bowen and myself were to be the comedians and the show's creator, Johnnie Hamp, was to host the evening. Classic footage from the original TV show was to be shown on a big screen. But things didn't go smoothly. Frank had to pull out due to ill health and then Jim Bowen suffered a stroke. So Roy Walker and Duggie Brown were brought in.

We filmed the show and, coupled with a documentary, "The 40th Anniversary of The Comedians Live" was released. I have to say, Paul did a great job on that DVD. He was very hands on, and took great care in making sure that it was perfect. I for one am very happy with the way it turned out. If you want a copy, just go to my website where it can be ordered.

The great thing about the summer of 2011 was that Tony Jo had moved his Summer Shows to Blackpool Grand Theatre and asked me to be the special guest on Joe Longthorne's show. I was only too happy to do it because, in my opinion, Joe is about the best entertainer we have ever produced in the UK. He was doing two nights at The Grand, so I was lucky enough to be working at the same venue for three nights.

Joe's fans are incredible. They follow him everywhere and several of them book front row seats at every show. They bring gifts and flowers to present to him at the end of his performance. To be honest, this worried me, as I knew that they only wanted to see their hero. So I made the decision to keep altering my set every show. I would keep putting new material in, which was good for me as it kept my mind working. It seemed to work because, at the end of the season, they gave me gifts to thank me for entertaining them over the summer months.

Shortly after the end of the Blackpool shows I was working on a cruise ship in the Mediterranean. Steve phoned me to tell me that he had agreed for me to perform at a charity show in Salford (Manchester). The date of the show was right in the middle of a busy period of work and was on my only day off. I told Steve that I would rather have had that day off, but he informed me that everything had been agreed and I would have to do the charity show. He told me that there would be a few big names there and that the charity would be represented by somebody called Anne. I have to admit that I wasn't really up for doing it, but as Steve had agreed to it, I was committed.

Steve then told me that the show had a name and asked if I wanted to know what it was. I said. "Yes," and he said, "It's called The Royal Variety Show." I was totally gobsmacked. This was incredible news. Every entertainer wants to perform on this show. Steve then explained that I had been booked as a "Theatre Only" act and wouldn't be included in the TV edit, but I was happy with that. At least I would be performing on The Royal Variety Show in front of Princess Anne. He went on to explain that they needed to fill in some time between magicians, Penn & Teller and the cast of "Singin' in the Rain". This was to allow enough time to build the set, which included water tanks.]

On my return, Steve and I discussed what I should put in my set, as I only had eight minutes to perform. The producers had asked that I included the Noddy routine, so I had to make sure that the rest of my time was made up of good strong material: I wanted to make a good impression.

On the day of the show we were told to be at The Lowry Theatre in Salford at 8.00am for rehearsals. On our arrival Steve and I were issued with our "Backstage Passes" and shown to the dressing room. As we walked in, a very tall gentleman greeted us, followed a smaller man: it was Penn &Teller. I got the shock of my life when Teller actually talked, something he never does on stage. Jason Manford, Tim Minchin and other comedians arrived and, by 9.00am, the room was full, we were all chatting and having a laugh. But other entertainers were much more serious. Barry Manilow had two dressing rooms opposite ours and when I went into the corridor to find a toilet, the one right next to our room had a sign on it saying, "For the sole use of Mr. Barry Manilow," which I found quite funny.

Rehearsals for the 1st half of the show went on until lunchtime, then after a short break, the 2nd half was rehearsed during the afternoon. Steve and I sat in the auditorium and watched as things progressed. Barry Manilow took to the stage and performed his two songs on a moving piano! He got a round of applause from the cast and crew who were watching. Then came the moment I was waiting for, Tony Bennett. He had brought his small band with him and walked on stage looking every inch the star that he is. He looked so at ease as he started to sing and was amazing. When he finished his set we all stood up and cheered. It was a privilege to have been part of this small gathering witnessing his genius.

With rehearsals over we grabbed some tea and prepared for the show. As part of the deal for agreeing to do the show for free, I was given one complimentary ticket. The face value was well over £300 and I wasn't going to give it up, but nobody wants to go on their own. Wendy was the first to refuse, so I remembered that Gill Isles who was the producer of "IDEAL" loved variety shows. She always came to Blackpool to see as many as she could. I called her up to ask her what she was doing on the day of the royal show and it turned out that she was in London for a meeting. When I told her that I had a ticket for The Royal Variety Show, she said she would get the meeting over as quickly as possible and get an earlier train back. She was over the moon and even bought a new dress for the occasion.

Peter Kay was the host for the evening and he did a fantastic job. Backstage was crawling with police, but some people still felt the need to have security men at their dressing room doors. X Factor winner, Leona Lewis had a guy sat on a chair by her door. Former Pussycat Dolls singer, Nicole Sherzinger had a bigger guy stood in front of her door. Singer Cee Lo Green had a couple of huge guys wandering around outside his door. Both Barry Manilow and Tony Bennett had large entourages around them wherever they went. I don't know what they thought might happen to them.

The show started and I was quite relaxed, but as my time came closer, my nerves began to kick in. Penn & Teller performed a trick with goldfish, which left the audience stunned. It was now my turn and a voice-over made the announcement, "And now, please welcome Mick Miller." I walked on stage and immediately felt at ease. I was getting big laughs and my eight minutes went by all too quickly.

Back in the dressing room one of the production team thanked me and told me that I was now free to leave the theatre because, as I was a "theatre only" act, I wouldn't be in the finale and wouldn't be introduced to Princess Anne. I knew this was the deal from the start, but I was still a bit disappointed. Still, I had realised an ambition, by performing at The Royal Variety Show.

A few days later I was working in London at a luncheon. We had decided to go on the train and avoid the traffic madness in the run up to Christmas. Whilst we were travelling down, Steve's phone rang. As he chatted he looked at me and smiled. It was the producer of the Royal Variety Show and she wanted permission to use my spot in the TV edit. Apparently, the TV executives had been viewing the footage and had decided that my act was just too good to leave out. Of course, Steve agreed and I was indeed included in the TV version.

When the show went out a couple of weeks later, my facebook, Twitter and e-mail went mad. I also had phone calls from people like Jethro and Bobby Davro congratulating me on my performance. It also wasn't long before Tony Jo got in touch to see if I would be interested in headlining my own show at Blackpool Grand Theatre during the summer of 2012.

Lots of things are happening and, at 62, I am still full of ambition. I have read for a part in a new BBC sitcom and am hopeful that I might be able to reprise the role of Keith in the film version of IDEAL. I've never been happier and I'm looking forward to whatever life brings. As I write this I have just started my Blackpool summer shows with The Comedians and my own Comedy Bonanza show. I am about to go up to Edinburgh to perform at the famous Fringe Festival and have a relatively full work diary.

Wendy and I are still together after all these years. I don't know how she puts up with me, but she does. She hasn't read any of this book during the writing stage, as she wants to enjoy it as a finished product. So, I hope she enjoys reading it to the very end because I'm dedicating it to her to thank her for her love and support. Which leaves me just one thing to say:

Wendy, I love you, will you marry me?

ND - #0027 - 051120 - C16 - 234/156/10 - PB - 9781780354552 - Gloss Lamination